SNOW ANGELS ON THE MOON

RUSSIE LANE

Snow Angels on the Moon
Copyright © 2019 Russie Lane

ISBN: 978-1-63381-197-3

All rights reserved. No part of this book may be reproduced in any
form or by any electronic or mechanical means, including information
storage and retrieval systems, without permission in writing from the
author, except by a reviewer, who may quote brief passages in review.

Designed and Produced by
Maine Authors Publishing
12 High Street, Thomaston, Maine 04861
www.maineauthorspublishing.com

Printed in the United States of America

In memory of my father, who has been my biggest supporter throughout my life, whether it be playing Little League or following my dreams. He has always encouraged me to write a book, but I bet he never thought it would be about him.

TABLE OF CONTENTS

INTRODUCTION IX
1 NOTHING LIKE MY FATHER 1
2 PAVLOV'S DOG 9
3 CALL ME ODD 17
4 DAD'S VOICE 23
5 AWAKE IN THE NIGHT 29
6 A LITTLE MIFFED 39
7 TWO WORDS 47
8 FACING GOLIATH 55
9 BOOTHBAY HISTORICAL 63
10 A GAME CHANGER 71
11 DOCK THE DAMN BOAT! 77
12 MOUNTING PILES 83
13 GO WEST, YOUNG MAN 87
14 BEST FRIENDS 93
15 THE ROAD *LES* TRAVELED 101
16 A WONDERFUL GIFT 109
17 WHEN IT RAINS, IT POURS 121
18 A TALE OF TWO ISLANDS 127
19 BACK WHERE I BEGAN 137
20 EVERYBODY NEEDS A NAME 143
21 ON HOLD 149
22 A PLACE ONCE CALLED HOME 159
23 THE UNREST OF THE STORY 167
24 WHERE THE MAGIC HAPPENS 173
25 FROZEN 179
26 OH ME FATHER WAS A KEEPER 185
27 AN OPEN PALM 191
28 A TINGE OF RED 197
29 FINALLY, A FILM FESTIVAL 203
30 GETTING MY BEARINGS 211

INTRODUCTION

My father always said he wasn't a hero, but a newspaper clipping tucked away in an old family album told a different story. It spoke of five young campers rescued from an overturned sailboat off the Maine coast in 1958. If not for the intervention of a lightkeeper, all five souls would have surely perished. That keeper was my father.

All but forgotten, the story resurfaced some fifty-seven years later. When questioned about the event, my father was hard-pressed to provide many details. In his defense, it did happen a very long time ago. Determined as I was to find out what had become of those five saved campers, I did face obstacles that made me an unlikely candidate for the job of investigative journalist.

The battle was on...not just against time and my father's fading memory, but with my role as a reluctant storyteller. A lifelong stutterer, I preferred hiding in the shadows, adopting Abraham Lincoln's words: "It is better to remain silent and be thought a fool, than to speak out and remove all doubt." I had no problem with remaining silent; it seemed like a perfect strategy.

As we go through life, however, we cannot be silent in all situations. What if someone needs help? You've got to pick up the phone and call 9-1-1. What if you see someone being treated unfairly? You need to take a stand and be a voice for justice. And what if you have a story that both touches the heart and is full of lessons? It needs to be told.

Armed with the lone news article, I set out to uncover the details of that long-ago August afternoon. My mission soon transformed into a calling that had me discovering as much about my father and myself as about the people I was searching for.

Signed,
A Reluctant Storyteller

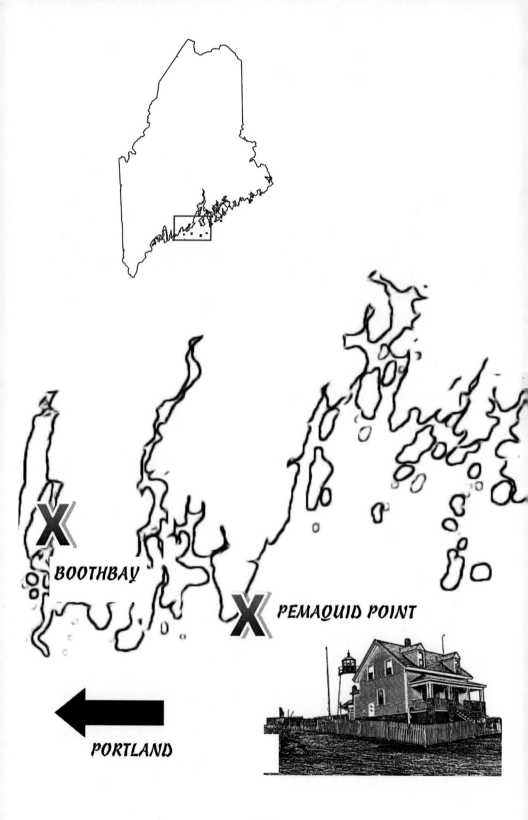

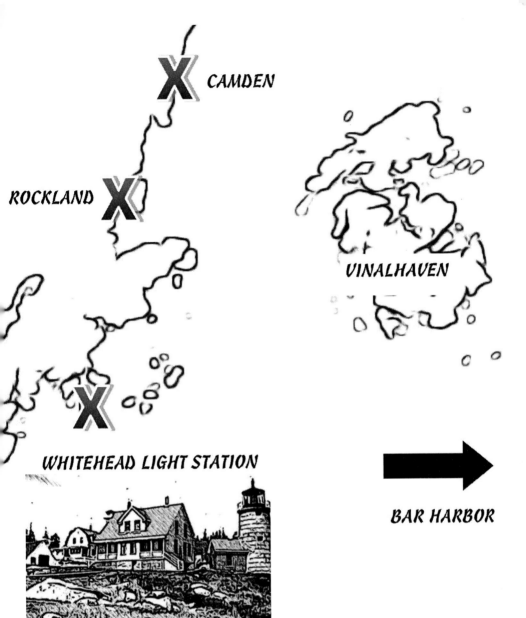

CHAPTER 1

NOTHING LIKE MY FATHER

Before stepping out of the truck, I couldn't help but feel a little guilty. The fresh coating of snow that had lightly fallen most of the afternoon made the world look new again. The aftermath was typical Maine, a picturesque scene that begged me to go away, leaving it undisturbed. Even the landscape, like the staunch natives who inhabit it, can be a wee bit too standoffish some days. I wondered if the Sea of Tranquility treated Neil Armstrong in the same fashion before he walked on the moon. How silly of me to make such a comparison. Maybe it was my tiredness or the feeling of being beaten down by the world, but tonight I was looking for a little inspiration from one of my childhood heroes.

The clouds opened like a curtain on a stage to reveal the colorful evening sky. It most certainly would usher in the cold temperatures along with it. Seeing the last few glimpses of sunlight reflecting across the ice-covered cove would be worth the extra couple of logs on the fire. It made for an exquisite backdrop for what lay on the shoreline. There stood the brick and mortar of Miles Memorial Hospital, a place I knew well. After all, I was born there. Over the years, I had returned more often than I wanted to, forever in need of stitches, a cast for a broken limb, or to check on a sick loved one. The latter being my purpose tonight.

Between me and my destination lay a pristine snow-covered sidewalk, a barrier for the tired old man that I was fast becoming. One who worries about the ice lurking in wait to sweep him off his feet, and not in a good way. And yet a blank canvas to the little boy that still resides somewhere deep inside me. If given a chance, he would spring to life, dashing through that fresh blanket of snow, zigzagging his way to the hospital. Of course, the little boy couldn't help but stop every now and again to make his mark on the world—a trail of snow angels. Tonight, though, is not a good night for such joviality. We can play someday soon, I promise. With that, the little boy in me subsided.

"That's one small step for man..." With one giant leap, I planted both feet firmly in the snow. Hearing the truck door slam behind me was a reminder that we'd soon be closing the door on 2014. I, for one, was not going to shed any tears over its passing. I couldn't. My quota for the year had already been depleted. In a one–two punch that brought our family to its knees, death had hit home closer than it ever had before. In the springtime, my father-in-law lost his nine-month battle with brain cancer. Then, along with the falling leaves of autumn, came devastating news that our daughter, five months along with our first grandchild, had lost her baby. Now, with only weeks left until the start of the new year, we were more than ready to finish 2014 and send it packing.

I wasn't sure what to expect next as I navigated a straight line up the sidewalk toward the hospital. Dad had been admitted earlier in the week fighting pneumonia; to compound matters, my mother was back at home wrestling with the same ailment. Neither one seemed to be making much headway at getting better. At eighty-three, Dad had us concerned. He had been spending more than his fair share of time at the hospital over the past few years, and on several different occasions, we feared we were going to lose him.

The automatic doors swung wide as I approached the entrance and stomped my way inside. I left my calling card—a pile of snow—on the welcome mat. Stepping off the rug and onto the highly polished floor, the soles of my wet boots screeched, "Look at me! Look at me!" My boots were certainly not speaking on my behalf. With each step, I attempted to silence the alarm coming from my heels. Changing my gait from an abnormally wide stride to walking on tippy-toes (and everything in between) proved to be of no help. My boots still screamed for attention. I turned a few heads that day, but not for my grace or good looks. What's that saying? The squeaky wheel gets the grease. That evening I discovered the squeaky boots get the attention, as well.

2

NOTHING LIKE MY FATHER

Fortunately, I had opted out of sneaking Dad's poodle, Oakie, into the hospital for a visit. There is just something about a boy and his dog that warms the heart and soothes the soul. A visit from Dad's best friend could do more for his health than any pill, but the tension between my boots and the floor would most certainly have blown our cover. Approaching Dad's room, I heard a familiar laugh spill out into the hallway. That was a good sign. Turning the corner, I quickly tapped twice on Dad's door as a courtesy and walked on in. *Squeak-squeak-squeak.*

Dad was sitting up in a chair. An attractive young nurse was changing his bedding. He was all smiles and she was still chuckling, obviously from something he had said. What a great surprise! Dad wasn't just out of bed, he was laughing and entertaining the nurses. He had bounced back once again!

"You are having way too much f-f-fun in here. You won't want to leave," I joked as I shrugged off my coat (along with my difficulty in forming the *f* sound). Sitting down in the chair opposite my father, I laid my coat across my lap.

"Oh, we would keep him right here if it were up to us," the nurse offered, tugging at the corners of the sheets.

To that Dad remarked that if he could have a pretty nurse like her make his bed every day, he would consider staying longer. Her smile widened. With a lull in the conversation, Dad took the opportunity to introduce us. "This is my son, Russ Junior."

"Ah, yes, I see the resemblance," she acknowledged with a nod of her head.

"That's where it stops. I am nothing like my father." My response was automatic.

"And I am some damn glad of that," Dad chimed in with an approving grin to second the motion.

The nurse looked up unamused. "You're nothing like your father?" Her question hung in the air. Hearing my words parroted back to me, I regretted voicing them. "That's too bad; we could use more men like your dad." A stern look took over her face and her smile dissipated. Her eyes narrowed into little slits as she scolded me in silence. Her

SNOW ANGELS ON THE MOON

mouth stopped moving, but her thoughts were coming through loud and clear: What kind of son are you? How can you say something like that about your father? Who do you think you are?

Her telepathy bombarded me. I tried to explain, but she wouldn't let me get a thought in edgewise. So I just sat there and took the mental abuse. Finishing the bed, she gathered the dirty linen (along with whatever was left of my ego) and whisked past me. At the door, she turned and we made eye contact. She wasn't finished with me yet. The fear of frostbite became all too real as she continued to chastise me through her icy glare. Then, glancing at Dad, both her face and tone softened. "Ring the bell if you need anything, Dearie. I'll check in later."

With that, she turned on her heels and disappeared. I fought the urge to get up out of my chair, follow her into the hallway and try to explain that I really was a good son. Realizing she would never understand, I turned my attention back to my father.

"Glad to see you're up and around, Dad. You had us p-p-p-pretty worried." My mouth got tangled on the *p*, but I wrestled with the sound, forcing out puffs of air until I was victorious.

He responded with a question: "Where's your mother?"

Dad didn't wait for my answer. The crime show he was fixated on was in the middle of a commercial break, and for some reason he needed to explain the episode. I halfheartedly listened to the details, completely tuning him out at the gory parts. His words turned to mumbles as I became lost in my own thoughts.

The nurse's comments had struck a chord. She was right. The world did need more men like Dad. She just didn't understand where I was coming from with my words. Throughout my whole life, I had secretly looked up to my father, but it was entirely against what he preached. "Don't be like me, Son. Go make something of yourself." From day one he had trained me well—a little bit too well.

The commercial ended and my father stopped talking as he went into his usual television trance. The show was riveting—at least to him—and he needed to know how it ended. I sat quietly so as not to interrupt while my eyes centered on him. This frail figure of a man, who was once bigger than life, seemed to be swallowed up by the chair.

4

Dad had a tough life growing up in one of the poorer families in town. His father was a lobster fisherman. His mother had all she could do to keep up with cooking and laundry for their fourteen children. Sadly, they lost two children during infancy and one girl, Mary, barely three years old, went to sleep after eating poison berries and never woke up. Dad was pretty much raised by his siblings half the time and left to fend for himself the other half. No one seemed to care the day he quit high school. He worked at odd jobs until old enough to join the Navy at the start of the Korean War.

Later, in January 1952, while crossing the wintry North Atlantic on a tin-can destroyer, Dad experienced a tragedy that would haunt him for the rest of his days. The USS *William M. Wood* had sailed headfirst into a raging storm that had the hardiest of sailors retreating to their bunks. It would be a crossing that would find many vessels in distress far out in the Atlantic. Chatter over the ship's radio even spoke of the *Queen Mary*, a ship almost three times the size of my father's destroyer, also struggling in the heavy seas.

Fiercely pounded by wind and waves, Dad's ship rolled to her side a terrifying fifty-eight degrees. Dishes in the galley came crashing to the floor. One of their lifeboats broke away from its rigging and was swept overboard. Dad, along with some of the crew, was sent outside to resecure the remaining equipment. My father looked up just in time to see a large wave crash against the hull where his best friend, Billy L'Heureux, was working. The wall of water cleared the deck of everything that wasn't tied down, Billy included. The gut-wrenching cry of "MAN OVERBOARD!" rang throughout the ship as the engines backed down.

On deck, the crew ran to see if there was anything they could do. They all knew the answer before they got there. Hanging over the rail, Dad looked down to see his buddy being pushed away by the wake of the ship's momentum. Desperately calling out for help, Billy's cries were gathered by the wind and thrown back to the sea. Locking eyes, my father saw Billy's face fill with terror. The crew could do nothing but watch helplessly as the ocean drew back, amassing itself into an angry fist. It exploded on top of Billy's head in a fury that no one could have survived. Heart-wrenching, yet mercifully, when the wave was gone, so was Billy.

Horrified, Dad couldn't imagine what could be worse than watching his best friend wash overboard. He didn't have to wait long to discover the answer. Looking up, he saw the shock and disbelief on the sailor's all-too-familiar face standing next to him. It was Raymond L'Heureux, Billy's brother.

No one slept much that night or for quite a few nights after that. Eventually, Dad stopped crying himself to sleep in his bunk. Months later, the nightmares ceased their nightly assault and surfaced sporadically. What never stopped, however, was Dad's determination. He vowed never to feel that helpless again.

After Dad's Navy years, he enlisted in the Coast Guard. Most of his time was spent manning lighthouses off the coast of Maine. He married my mother, Sandra Miller, and they decided to have two kids, my sister (Becky) and me. After five years, Dad left the Coast Guard and my folks returned to raise their family in the little village of Pemaquid in Midcoast Maine. Like so many down through the generations, Dad turned to the ocean for his livelihood. Following in his father's footsteps, he became a lobster fisherman. It's what they knew; it's what they did. Throughout his life, Dad maintained the reasoning for his career choice: He "didn't have enough brains to amount to much else." However, I knew better.

Now, years later, I sat in the hospital observing him. I must admit he did not look bad for his age. But even with a mostly full head of dark hair, you could tell that time and sickness were taking their toll. Maybe he'd been sick for so long that his body had been preserved by inactivity.

My mother took her wedding vows seriously. She waited on Dad in sickness and in health, and then in more sickness. She was a saint in everyone's eyes except his. Now, exhausted and sick herself, she was getting some much-needed rest. In an odd way, having Dad in the hospital was a good thing.

Finally, at the next commercial, I caught enough of Dad's attention to answer his question from ten minutes before. "Oh, Mom is getting a little better, but she's too sick to come to the hospital." My words sounded funny as I repeated them in my mind: *too sick to come to the hospital.*

"It figures; she just wants to get away from me. I bet she's not even sick at all." Dad's words were seasoned with an unexplained bitterness.

"Dad, she's a lot sicker than you are!" I stood my ground and defended my mother's honor. "In fact, she should probably be in the hospital instead of you." The more I spoke, the more sense it made, at least to me. "And, yes, she needs a little time away from you, just like you do from her. Maybe you'll appreciate each other a little bit more." I never noticed throughout the impassioned speech that I hadn't stuttered once. Funny how defending your mother's honor brings out the orator in all of us.

As my rant turned to logic, Dad muted the TV and seemed to let my words soak in. They must have appeared reasonable because instead of perpetuating the myth about my mother, he brought out the white flag, surrendering with, "You are a good son."

I smiled. Now, if only that nurse was around to hear Dad's comment.

We talked for a while with the TV muted. I don't really remember what we chatted about. It didn't matter. It just felt good to know that talking to me was taking priority over watching the ending of his crime show. (Later in the conversation, he would confess that he had seen the program several times before.) Well, having his full attention felt good for a little while anyway.

Reaching down to check that my boots were dry, I knew it was safe to go. We said our goodbyes and I made my way to the door. Dad's TV was off mute and blasting again as I peered around the corner to be sure the coast was clear. To my delight, the hallway was empty. This time my boots were silent as I walked past the nurses' station. Still in enemy territory, I needed to make it to the stairwell to escape with what was left of my dignity. Looking straight ahead, I avoided making eye contact with anyone. After all, I had drawn enough attention to myself for one day.

Just when I thought I had made a clean getaway, my father's nurse emerged from the room ahead of me. Had she been waiting to ambush

SNOW ANGELS ON THE MOON

me? I froze in my tracks. This time, though, her eyes remained soft and caring. She smiled a genuine smile as she said, "Your dad is doing great!"

"Thanks for all you've done." I felt relieved; all had been forgiven.

Leaving her to her duties, I made my way down the staircase and back out the entrance. Finding the same tracks in the snow that I'd left on the way in, I followed them back to my truck. One step coming in now equaled three steps going out. Had my steps shortened up that much? Like playing a game, I became more deliberate in swinging my arms and widening my stride to reach my earlier footprints.

Once inside the truck, I set the defroster on high. Now there was nothing to do but shiver from the biting cold and wait for the windshield to clear. Not the warmest accommodation for a little time to myself, but it was worth the trade-off. Besides, if it was *too* cozy, I might fall asleep right here for the evening. I guess burning the candle at both ends was starting to catch up with me.

CHAPTER 2

PAVLOV'S DOG

With the windshield finally clear, it was on to Biscay Pond and my next patient. I prepared to head in the wrong direction. The hospital's entrance, located between two hills, demanded it. The long, steep hill to the right leads to my hometown of Bristol; the smaller incline off to the left goes to Damariscotta. The decision on which direction one should turn is dictated more by the season than by the destination. The icy roads of winter make a right turn up Hospital Hill darn near impossible. Conversely, waiting to make a left turn in the heavy summer traffic can test the patience of Job. So, like it or not, although I wanted to turn right to get to my parents' home, I took a left turn toward "Scotty." The plan was to drive into town, reverse direction, and get a running start up Hospital Hill. That's how life can be sometimes. The right decision might take you away from your intended destination, at least for a little way.

Before I go any further, I should explain that Scotty is not a person, it's a place. Well, more like a nickname. It's short for Damariscotta. The locals toggle back and forth between the two names, depending on the circumstances. It's like your mother calling out to you: So long as she uses your first name alone, everything is fine. However, if she addresses you by your full, formal name—the one that you have only seen written out on your birth certificate—that's when you know you're in trouble. The uses of *Damariscotta* and *Scotty* are quite similar. I think it's the only town in Maine with a swear word built right in. Maybe that's why when you go to the dentist or get snarled up in traffic there, everyone calls it "Damariscotta." On the other hand, when it's something good, such as finding a dollar bill on the sidewalk or going for ice cream, that can only happen in "Scotty." It has gotten to the point where you can

SNOW ANGELS ON THE MOON

tell what type of day people are having by which name they use. If my mother says she went to Scotty, I know she had a good day. However, if she says she went to Damariscotta, I am quick to offer condolences.

Before I could make the turn and head back out of town, a growl came from somewhere inside the truck. It sounded like my dog, Baxter. But it couldn't be; he was ten miles down the peninsula hibernating at home. It didn't sound like a mean growl, just a hungry one. He does that when I forget to feed him. He will patiently sit in front of me attempting to make eye contact. If he goes unnoticed, he will start a series of low growls as if clearing his throat: "Excuse me...excuse me...I hate to bother you, but..." Finally, if that still fails to get my attention, he will escalate his efforts to the next level. One lone bark followed by several clearing-his-throat growls. (As far as my obedience training is concerned, he has done a good job in teaching me his commands.)

There it goes again! This time I didn't just hear it, I felt it. The growl was clearly coming from inside my belly. Looking at the clock on the truck's dashboard, I realized my stomach had a right to complain. It was way past suppertime. Never one to question the demands of my internal organs, I changed course for the McDonald's drive-thru.

Pulling into line with two other cars, I suddenly had a vision of being back in school waiting my turn to speak. Growing up, my speech problem manifested itself in everything I did. Like Pavlov's dog, the sound of a ringing telephone would trigger a response; mine was a cold sweat in lieu of Rover's salivating. When it came to school, my heart would beat wildly as the teacher went up and down the rows asking each student a question. The agony of anticipating my turn to speak was almost too much to bear. As the teacher approached, I would work myself into a frenzy. The result? I'd either freeze or—perhaps worse— repeatedly force air past my lips in an effort to expel any word from my mouth. I couldn't have cared less whether I gave the right answer or not; all that mattered was getting the nightmare over with. Either way, my response usually was greeted with chuckles from around the room and a stern glare from the teacher to the offending individuals.

Buying into the old adage "if you can't beat 'em, join 'em," I started using the snickering to my advantage. I discovered that the silliest fluent answer would yield the biggest amount of laughter. By striking first blood with humor, I could beat those who might make fun of me to the punch. More often than not, the laughter put me at ease, at least enough to follow up with the right answer minus the stuttering. The downside: My teachers repeatedly scolded me for not taking my studies seriously. If they only knew. It wasn't the studies that concerned me; it was about verbally surviving the moment, and I took *that* very seriously. But to argue my defense would only necessitate another attempt at speaking, and I certainly was not going there.

As I now waited my turn at McDonald's, that same fear of speaking resurfaced. With dimming brake lights, the car in front of me moved on to the payment window. Slowly, I eased up to the drive-thru speaker as if cautiously approaching a dangerous animal. There was an eerie silence as I peered at the microphone and waited to be acknowledged. Oblivious to my present-day surroundings, my mind took me back in time to when I was a little boy.

Standing at a soda fountain, I was looking up at a gentleman behind the counter. "May I help you?" he inquired with a kind voice. My heart pounded so hard I thought it might rip uncontrollably out of my chest. I froze in fear; if I could have turned and run, I would have. This was speech therapy at eight years old. Minutes before, I had been up the street for my weekly visit at the Pine Tree Society for Crippled and Handicapped Children. That's a mouthful for anyone, with or without a speech problem. The name didn't help the self-esteem of anyone in need of their services. I didn't feel crippled, but maybe I was. My speech therapist led me out of her office, down a corridor past scores of pictures of kids with twisted legs wearing braces. Thankfully, we bypassed the conference room where the group speech therapy took place. I was glad not to be going in there. Three-quarters of those sessions were spent watching each other struggle at introducing ourselves. Whoever thought that Misery Loves Company Speech Therapy was a good idea, I'll never know.

As we left the confines of the building, my therapist reached down and grabbed my hand. Not in a motherly way, but more as if I was being escorted to the principal's office. Walking up the street to the drugstore, I couldn't help but drag my feet just a little. I felt like a condemned man being led to the gallows. Once inside, she handed me a dollar bill and pointed toward the soda fountain. Taking my place in line behind only one other person, it really wasn't much of a line, but I welcomed it to allow me time to catch my breath. The speech therapist retreated, stationing herself back by the door to block any chance of my escape. Alone and afraid, my mission was playing over and over in my head. It seemed simple enough: make my way to the counter and somehow order my last meal, a strawberry shake.

The person ahead of me was done too soon. Taking one step forward as if volunteering for a suicide mission, I met the challenge head-on. Evidently, during the commotion of stepping forward, I had missed the gentleman's greeting. There was an awkward silence.

"May I help you?" he repeated. This time he was a little louder. Thinking back now, it was not forceful, just louder. As a kid, it is sometimes hard to tell the difference. I panicked. Like pulling the plug from the bathtub drain, everything I had learned in speech therapy to that point disappeared.

"May I p-p-please have a sh-sh..." With my lungs depleted of air, I inhaled a deep breath and tried again. Thinking things couldn't get much worse, I had my first introduction to Murphy's Law. The bell on the shop's door rang out as it swung open. Pivoting around, I saw two bigger kids enter and make a beeline for the soda fountain. They stopped only a few inches behind me. Coins jingling in their pockets said they were in a hurry. Turning back toward the counter, I felt more pressure than ever. Their giggling from behind only added to the anxiety that was now reaching a fever pitch. As I attempted to speak again, I knew it wasn't going to be pretty. If only life had dealt me an easier task, such as climbing Mt. Everest or storming the beaches of Normandy.

"May I help you?" It took a minute for my head to decipher the garbled voice coming from the speaker. Of course, it didn't help that my mind had me jumping back and forth over forty-something years between a drugstore soda fountain and a present-day McDonald's drive-thru.

"Yes, you may," I responded, followed by silence. My tongue lay life-less, sulking at the bottom of my mouth. Just like so many years before, it wanted a strawberry shake. Only one small problem: It would have to perform to get one. Pronouncing s words have always proven diffi-cult for me. It seems ironic that my favorite drink is a strawberry shake. And yes, if life and words aren't cruel enough, my next favorite is a Shamrock Shake.

Having been down this road before, I knew there were safer things to order on the menu. Some days, though, you just want what you want. I decided right at that moment to go for it. My tongue perked up its ears. I stared intently at the microphone just outside my window. My tongue sat quietly waiting for a treat. The airflow rushing past my lips was barely making a sound.

"What did you say, sir? I couldn't hear that." The speaker came to life.

"I'd like a st-st-straw...b-b-berry...sh-sh..."

"Sorry, sir, can you move closer to the microphone. You are breaking up."

I knew that would be of no help, but I followed the instructions anyway. Poking my head further out the truck window, I stretched my neck to get as close to the microphone as possible. A car pulled up behind me, seemingly in a hurry, but that was probably just my interpretation. Here, at age fifty-four, things didn't seem much differ-ent from when I was eight years old. Surrendering, I knew the joy of a strawberry shake would not be mine that evening.

"Can I have a number eight please?" I asked, defeated. The disap-pointment in my voice had to be more than evident. I was ordering in a question, not a statement. What if the voice on the other end said no? What would I do then, drive off? Heck, I couldn't even remember what a number eight was. All I knew was that I was getting one whether I liked it or not.

"Would you like a Coke with that?" the speaker asked.

"Yes, please," I answered, grateful for the suggestion. Soon the trans-action was complete, and I was back in gear barreling past the hospital entrance and on up the hill toward my parents' place. Conquering the icy hill soothed my battered self-esteem. It really had taken a beating all evening. Reaching into the McDonald's bag, I was anxious to see what I had ordered for dinner. It really didn't matter, though. My belly was saying that anything at this point would be a happy meal. Clicking the phone button on my steering wheel, I uttered the words, "Call home." It was time to check in with my wife.

"Hello," Heidi answered with a smile. You didn't have to see her to know it was there; you could hear it in her voice.

"Hello. This is your husband. Remember me?" I half joked. It was as though my words were one of those half medallions people wear around their necks.

"Just barely," she chuckled back with the other half. A perfect match.

Heidi was a summer girl who hailed from Northern Maine— Millinocket, to be exact. Her family would come to the coast after school let out in June. She worked at a local restaurant until just before Labor Day, when they would migrate north again for the winter. Some might consider them to be confused snowbirds.

I was a man in uniform—not military, but that of a park ranger. It was my first year in college, and I loved my summer job. Armed with a badge and a lawn mower, I kept the grounds of Colonial Pemaquid, a state historic site. Our first date was going out in my father's boat to do my second job, tending lobster traps. After watching me haul the first two traps, Heidi found an extra pair of gloves on the dashboard. Without any coaxing, she soon had her hands dipping into the soupy fish guts and filling bait bags. I was in love. Thirty-three years and two grown kids later, we were still going strong.

As we talked on the phone, the time and miles flew by. We told each other about our day. My encounter with Dad's nurse and the strawberry shake–ordering fiasco were long forgotten. I was feeling better about myself. Heidi has a way of doing that for me. Coming down into Bristol Mills, I told her we were about to lose our connection.

"Well, in that case, good ni—"

The phone went silent as the speed limit dipped to 30 mph at the bottom of the hill. I had entered Bristol's Death Valley for cell phones. For some reason, losing my cell phone coverage through that half-mile stretch of road seemed okay. The fast pace of the world was left at the top of the hill. The dropped call acted as a gentle reminder to slow down through the village, and in the bigger scheme of things, maybe take life at a slower pace as well.

CHAPTER 3

CALL ME ODD

Turning down into my parents' driveway, I heard their two dogs sounding the alarm. If my mother hadn't been awake, she surely was now. They were opposites, these two canine companions, Andy and Oakie (more like Mutt and Jeff). Andy is an oversized border collie who dreams of being a lapdog. Oakie is a small poodle aspiring to be a Great Dane. Walking up the ramp leading to my folks' front door, I found it interesting that both dogs wouldn't bark at the same time. They were taking turns, like having a conversation.

"Did you hear something? Ruff, ruff?"

"Yes, I think it's a car driving in."

"Oh, maybe we should bark louder to alert the surrounding neighborhoods?"

"That's a great idea, Ruff, RUFF, *RUFF!*"

With tails wagging, all barking suddenly ceased as I entered the house. Both dogs met me at the door, each sniffing a different pant leg. It was like they didn't quite trust their eyesight and needed to get a good whiff for verification purposes. "Two forms of ID, please."

I poked my head into my mother's bedroom. She didn't just leave the TV blaring away like my father does, making conversation almost impossible. She turned it off.

"How's Dad doing?" she asked with a raspy, nearly nonexistent voice. Coughing into her elbow, she listened intently as I explained that he was getting back to his old self again. She was happy to hear the good news. I asked her how she was feeling. Ignoring the question about herself, like most mothers do, she diverted attention back to me. "Did you get something to eat?"

"Yup, I went to McDonald's in Damariscotta."

SNOW ANGELS ON THE MOON

"That doesn't sound very appetizing." Her eyes were sympathetic. In hindsight, I should have told her, "I went to McDonald's in Scotty."

Her progress on the road to recovery wasn't as rapid as Dad's, but then again, she was battling exhaustion as well. Many caregivers do. They spend so much time tending to their sick mate that they neglect themselves. I reminded her that I would be downstairs if she needed anything. Thanking me for spending the night again, she added how it got kind of spooky in the house all by herself.

Winding down the spiral staircase to the basement, I was hit head-on with what looked like a messy room. No worries. Nobody had broken in and ransacked the place. I was the lone perpetrator. It was part of the process. The room looked in disarray with stacks of photo albums of all shapes and sizes. However, they were strategically placed around the bed. I had been taking them from the closet and reliving family history. My system for tracking the photo albums was a good one. The dusty piles were the books yet to go over, while the clean ones could be returned to the closet. One special pile was set off to the side. This was my real reason for binge-thumbing through all my parents' pictures: the search for my Great-Aunt Pauline.

Family is what mattered most growing up. Call me odd, but if I had a choice between a box of twenty-dollar bills and one containing old family pictures, the latter would win every time. Who needs a box filled with the same picture of Andrew Jackson? This interest in my family history had been a seed that was planted from one of my earliest memories.

Some of my happiest times as a child were when my mother would make us a picnic lunch. We would load into the car and head to the end of Pemaquid Point. Eating on the rocks in the salt air gave the bologna sandwich a gourmet taste that I don't believe can be duplicated by the finest chefs from around the world. We would then bring out the binoculars and try to spot my father hauling traps somewhere on the bay.

On one such occasion, it was just my mother and me. I probably hadn't even started school yet. After we climbed into the car, I was surprised when my mother drove in the opposite direction, away from

18

the point. Soon we were winding our way over to Pemaquid Harbor. Driving past the post office, she tooted her horn. That's when I knew we weren't stopping. It wasn't something we would normally do at every post office, just the one at Pemaquid Harbor. It was during business hours, so odds were that my Aunt Ollie was inside working. And if she was working, odds were pretty good she was looking out the window. And if she was looking out the window, odds were even better she would have seen us driving by. And if she saw us drive by and not stop or toot our horn, she would think that was pretty odd. So, my mother played the odds and tooted.

The road curved to the right and the trees briefly disappeared, revealing a gull's-eye glimpse overlooking Pemaquid Harbor and out into John's Bay. The evergreens quickly populated both sides of the road again and hung over the top, forming a tunnel in the woods. As we entered it, the sun went into hiding until we popped out the other side, arriving at our destination. My mother gathered her things. With picnic basket in one hand and me in tow with the other, she followed the path that led to the back side of a weather-beaten cottage. Continuing, we made our way around front to a panoramic view of outer Pemaquid Harbor. We saw several boats hauling traps, but none were my father's. It still was a perfect place to have a picnic lunch down on the rocks. A screen door slammed, and we turned around to be greeted with a smile. It was that of my Great-Aunt Pauline. I didn't know she was born into "greatness" by virtue of being a relative. I just thought she was Great-Aunt Pauline because she was "great."

Inviting us into her cottage, she wanted to show us something that "little boys might be interested in." My eyes widened as she took us to a shelf containing some strange things. Explaining that the artifacts were from Africa, she showed me pieces of ivory from an elephant's tusk, and she let me touch a leopard skin. But the thing that grabbed my attention the most was the one thing she wouldn't let me touch—a large wooden mask that hung on the wall. It was too frightening to look at, yet I couldn't look away. Great-Aunt Pauline was right: She did have some things that little boys might be interested in. So much so that the intrigue has lasted this little boy a lifetime.

SNOW ANGELS ON THE MOON

Over the years, I discovered what an interesting life Great-Aunt Pauline had lived, well, at least the second half anyway. It was 1935, and it seemed that, at thirty-six, Pauline was destined to be a spinster. Educated and working as a dental hygienist, some would say she lived a humdrum existence for years scraping plaque off her patients' teeth. When she visited her parents in Maine, her father would tease her, saying that if she didn't stop looking a gift horse in the mouth, she might never find a husband.

Then one day it happened. A tall, handsome stranger with a perfect toothy white smile came into her life and swept her off her feet. The only problem was that he was set to go back to his position as financial advisor to the country of Liberia in West Africa. As he was preparing to leave, he had a crazy idea. In a few months, he would be in England. He could buy her passage on a steamship. They could marry and travel Europe. Then they would split their years between Pemaquid and Monrovia. Pauline answered with a resounding yes, and plans were set in motion.

World War II brought them separation once again as Ted wanted to keep his bride out of harm's way and she was sent back to Maine. Ted would make frequent trips to Washington to meet with the War Department and help with the Allied effort. All the while, Pauline and Ted corresponded. It was a love story for the ages, and I had all the letters. I had started writing a book about Great-Aunt Pauline dozens of times. The evenings spent down in my parents' basement going over old pictures rekindled my desire to tell Pauline and Ted's story. It was time to finish that book.

Now, kicking off my boots, I flopped down on the unmade daybed. Grabbing the next dusty book from the pile, I opened it to reveal pictures of my father's time in the Coast Guard. This really was *ancient* history. It would take five more years before my parents would come to their senses and have me. And, of course, there was no hope of finding Pauline in any of those pictures.

Like a speed reader, I flipped through the pages at an astounding rate, barely focusing on pictures. I merely wanted to get to the end and be able to put it in the "been there, done that" pile. That evening,

20

I came close to slamming the covers together and moving on to the next album. But I had promised myself I would let no stone (or page) go unturned until I found everything concerning Great-Aunt Pauline. Reaching the end of the album, I stopped and stared. There, taped to the back cover, was a neatly trimmed newspaper clipping. I had forgotten all about this rescue thing Dad had done. Carefully preserved, yet yellowed with age, the newsprint bore the headline that had always seemed more fitting for a children's book than a news article:

Chance Glance to Sea by Light Keeper Led to Rescue of Five from Upset Sailboat Wednesday

Such a singsongy title, one to make Dr. Seuss proud! It must have been years since I had seen the article, let alone read it. I continued reading.

The Coast Guardsman's habitual scanning of the seas off his lighthouse at Whitehead Island every time he goes outdoors saved the lives of five young people Tuesday afternoon.

It's a good thing I was reading to myself and not aloud. Technically, it wasn't a run-on sentence as much as it was a run-out sentence. Many more like that and it would have me running out of breath and hyperventilating into a paper bag. With the headline stating the rescue happened on a Wednesday and the first line of the story saying it happened on a Tuesday, it should have been the first red flag of many that the article was filled with inaccuracies. But I hadn't noticed the discrepancies yet.

The story was an interesting one. Coming out of the lighthouse, my father had spotted a capsized sailboat about a mile and a half off Whitehead Island. Acting quickly, Dad ordered his assistant to call the Coast Guard base at Rockland and get rescue boats coming. He then sprinted to the other side of the island where their small "20-footer" utility boat was kept. When he arrived, he encountered lobsterman David Gamage and enlisted his help. They jumped in Gamage's lobster boat and went out to find five teenage campers clinging to an overturned sailboat.

SNOW ANGELS ON THE MOON

When questioned about the event, Dad always denied being a hero. As a child, I had tried to persuade him differently. "But, Dad, you have the newspaper article to prove it!"

His answer always made it clear that his life was not one to be looked up to. "I'll never amount to nothing. Don't be like me, Son. Go make something of yourself." With that diversion, both the story and photo album were destined to lay dormant, gathering dust in my parents' closet as the decades slipped by.

Now, much older, I read the story with fresh eyes. I had never realized they were a group of teenagers from a summer camp in Boothbay, only a couple of peninsulas away. It was at that moment that I wondered what it had been like for them to be in the water. The news story became less about the rescuers and more about the people who had been rescued.

Dad had searched for David Gamage over the years but eventually had given up. I assumed it was because David was quite a lot older than Dad, and we figured he must have passed on. But what about these camp kids? They would only be in their seventies. Where were they now? My curiosity was piqued.

As I looked down the list of names in the article, my enthusiasm diminished a bit. Only one was local. Ah yes, Lewis, a good Boothbay name. If I could locate any of them, Leslie Lewis would be the one. As for Jeffrey Stewart, Susan Sherer, Daniel Granoff, and Peter Laylin, I had no idea where to even start. My life was too busy and finding these kids was sure to be a monumental task. There was no way I was up for the challenge. Who was I to make a big deal about the rescue anyway? It was a dead story, declared so by the Coast Guard and seconded by my father. Like pulling the sheet back over a corpse, I closed the photo album. Besides, I thought, 2015 is the year to finish the book about Great-Aunt Pauline. So I added the Coast Guard album to the "been there, done that" pile and turned out the light.

CHAPTER 4

DAD'S VOICE

Desperate for a breath—any breath at all—I inhaled. Instead of air, my lungs filled with muddy water that churned up from the river bottom. Kicking my legs violently to reach the surface, I was well past the verge of panic. The more I flailed, the more the weeds tightened their grip on my extremities. My attempt to break free was futile. I was trapped. At that moment, all I could picture was my lifeless bloated body caught in the sea grass on the bottom of the Damariscotta River. Trying to float to the surface, I lay there, hovering like a grotesque balloon in the Macy's Thanksgiving Day Parade. Powerless, there was nothing I could do but wait for the divers to recover my body.

That vision gave what fight I had in me a second wind. I battled all the harder, refusing to die. It didn't take me long to knock all the pillows off the bed. Opening my eyes, I realized my legs were not tangled in weeds but in bed sheets. Trying to calm my rapidly beating heart, it was all I could do to convince myself it was just a dream. Still holding my breath for fear of drowning, I finally persuaded my lungs that conditions were okay for them to get back to work. I inhaled.

How could a dream seem so real? Maybe because it wasn't just a dream. Once upon a time, it was real, a terror from my past—something bad I had thought was buried for good—sneaking up on me in my deepest sleep. It was now as vivid and fresh as the memory of what I had for last night's dinner.

So, what on earth would cause this forty-year-old memory to jostle free and make its way to the top of my consciousness? The explanation seemed obvious. It had to have been triggered by reading the newspaper article on the rescue.

SNOW ANGELS ON THE MOON

Still shaking from the intense interruption of what had begun as a good night's sleep, I pulled the covers back up around me and lay there silently in the dark. As the sun appeared over the snowy treetops to light up a new day on Biscay Pond, I was still wide awake. Lying there, I became very aware of my heartbeat. It was irregular but kept repeating as if sending out a distress call to other ships at sea. There was no way I would be able to go back to sleep now. Trying to regain my composure, I closed my eyes and thought happy thoughts. But my mind wasn't buying it. Memories of the horror of that day came tumbling back in sequence, like dominoes.

Dad hated canoes, especially anywhere near the ocean. He always said the sea was unstable enough on its own. At the age of seventeen, like most teenage boys, I considered myself to be pretty much bullet-proof.

It was my senior year of high school, and I knew everything there was to know about everything. Thinking it would be fun to enter a canoe race, I floated the idea to one of my best friends, Fenton Lebon (I always like saying his name, *Fenton Lebon*). It was a hare-brained idea for two teenagers with no experience and no canoe. But ego and ignorance prevailed, so we came up with a canoe from somewhere and found ourselves frantically paddling at the start of the twelve-mile adventure. The course spanned the length of Damariscotta Lake and included two portages before ending in a tidal river leading to the ocean. It was a significant challenge for experienced paddlers, let alone two guys without a clue. This was my first time in a canoe, and if the river had had its way, it would have been my last.

Dad wasn't very happy about the idea. However, with the promise to wear my life jacket, he reluctantly was okay with it. Besides, I reassured him, I could dog-paddle with the best of them so there was really nothing to worry about. To be truthful, I was surprised he let me go, but even more surprised when Fenton Lebon's mother let him join in, too.

We started off strong and tired quickly. Although determined and deliberate with our strokes, we ended up traveling with a few other canoes bringing up the rear. It was a hot summer day, and we were working up quite a sweat. It was way too hot to wear a life jacket;

besides, it made a great seat cushion. As the day went on, my arms felt like jelly and my legs were cramping from sitting cross-legged in the canoe. If any of my limbs had been called into action to make a swimming motion, I am sure they would have failed miserably.

Neither one of us noticed as we portaged to the river that the water level was quite low. We had no idea what we were getting into. Had planning been part of the process, we would have known that the experienced racers would finish at high tide while the river was calm. We were, however, bringing up the rear on the back side of the tide. With a mile left to go, I stopped sitting on my life vest and threw it to the floor. It was my thought that a lower center of gravity would give us better stability for a fast finish. After a few moments, I heard my father's voice: "You had better put that on, Russie."

Looking down at the life jacket kicked aside at my feet, his words were clear, as if spoken right next to me. He'd even called me by name! I laid the paddle across my lap and donned the life jacket. Cinching it tight around my waist, I yelled to my buddy paddling in the front. Mimicking my father's instructions, I advised him, "You'd better put on your life jacket, Fenton."

It wouldn't be very long before we would find out that would be the best decision of our young lives. Rounding the next bend, we encountered a boiling cauldron of whitewater. This wasn't part of the plan (as if we even had one). The river was draining out in a hurry with the rushing tide. The canoe sped through the rapids with no assistance from us. Maybe this wasn't going to be as bad as I thought. The river was quick to disagree. We hit a rock and the current spun us around. Being young and inexperienced at paddling, we didn't stand a chance. We were out of control, merely terrified cargo. Like riding a bucking bronco, the tiny vessel first dipped down, then up, launching us into the air. Then, turning sideways, the force of the water flipped us upside down, emptying the canoe's entire contents into the river, us included.

My body was turning end over end doing cartwheels under water. Every so often, I would hit the river bottom and bounce along. With arms and legs flailing, I struggled to get to the surface. However, I didn't even know which way was up. Gulping for air, I found only muddy water. I fought back with every ounce of strength I could muster. No river was going to beat me.

Without warning, my body stopped its thrashing as the realization of my predicament took hold of my being. Fate had my full attention. There was no doubt about it: I was going to die. It was inevitable...and there was absolutely nothing I could do to prevent it.

The overwhelming panic disappeared. Everything became very still. In ultra-slow motion now, I stopped being dragged along the bottom. The river turned calm, releasing its death grip on me. A truce had been reached. Peace permeated my soul as my body gave up the struggle to survive. I felt my life leave. I was finished...

As quickly as the feeling of tranquility had appeared, it ended. Popping up to the surface, I shot out of the water like a newborn thrust out of the womb. The portion of river that had found its way into my lungs spewed back out through my nose. Coughing up something that would more aptly be described as muddy vomit, it felt as if all my insides wanted *out* of me. As the churning water continued to carry me down-river, I gradually realized I could breathe again! I never gave a thought to the life jacket holding me so snugly and quietly doing its job of keeping my head above water. Frantically, I searched for Fenton. While still gagging to clear my lungs, I twisted and contorted my body in circles looking for any sign of life in the water around me. I found none.

Can he really be gone? How can I face Fenton's mother with the news? With those thoughts, the real panic set in. Still caught in the clutches of the current, I was finally released into calmer waters. My feet happily touched the bottom, allowing me to stand. It felt like the hand of God had scooped me up and delivered me to the safety of shallow water. I had survived. Better yet, Fenton had, too. A few yards away, to my great relief, there he was, hanging onto the overturned canoe at the end of the rapids. I dog-paddled in his direction. Upon reaching the shoreline, the reunion was complete and we both laughed. My laughter had nothing to do with being amused. It was more to hide the fact that I was still shaking from one of the most terrifying experiences of my life.

Thoroughly soaked and exhausted, we watched from shore as the last two canoes successfully navigated the rapids. We had survived our foolishness that day with a degree of satisfaction in knowing that at least we weren't dead last. I was just grateful, at last, not to be dead.

Now, years later, lying in bed in my parents' basement, I was remembering in vivid detail the traumatic event. I was not sure what frightened me more: my near-death experience or the thought of losing my best friend and needing to face his mother. I did know one thing, though: It changed me. Before that day, living life meant taking it as it came—no shirt, no shoes, no problem. The experience showed me that life is precious and maybe I wasn't as indestructible as I had previously thought. I became more like my father that day, starting to anticipate and plan for what was around the next corner. Maybe it was what Dad had been trying to teach me all along. However, this was a lesson I had to learn on my own the hard way. Mind you, I am not complaining. Learning the hard way beats learning "too late" any day.

Looking at the clock, it was time to get ready for work. I put on my clothes and climbed up the spiral stairs. Stopping on the first few steps, I had the funny feeling I was forgetting something. My hands patted down my pockets while scanning the room. Reading glasses, yup. Wallet, check. Phone, got it. Everything was in its proper place. Over next to the bed, my eyes were drawn to the two stacks of photo albums, the completed pile and one to tackle tonight. My thoughts went back to those five teens. It dawned on me that I was more than a reader of their story. I, too, had spent time in the water and had been plucked out of the wet clutches of death by my father. Maybe not by his hand, but by his caring wisdom, wisdom passed down through the generations. It just happened to be my good fortune that I had heeded his words when I did.

I wondered what else I might have in common with the five campers. Had their experiences changed their lives, as well? Strangely, I felt a kindred spirit with them even though I had no idea who they were or what had become of them. Backing down the steps, I returned to the side of the bed and retrieved the album containing Dad's Coast Guard years from the "been there, done that" pile. I placed it down alone on the nightstand next to Great-Aunt Pauline's stack. One by one, I put the other photo albums back in the closet where they could gather more dust. Maybe it wouldn't be as difficult to find seventy-plus-year-old kids as I first had thought... As for telling Great-Aunt Pauline's story, after twenty-something years on the back burner, there was no harm in letting it simmer a little longer.

CHAPTER 5

AWAKE IN THE NIGHT

Over the next few days, my father came home from the hospital and my mother's health jumped right to the front. I was a little worried about Dad's dependency tiring her out and sending her into relapse, but honestly, having him home to wait on was all the medicine she needed.

As for me, I was chomping at the bit to find out more about the rescue. However, I waited for them to feel better before barraging them with questions. They both had gems to share about living on the island, but unfortunately, they couldn't provide many answers about the rescue. In their defense, it did happen a very long time ago. I had pinned my hopes on hearing the story straight from the horse's mouth. Instead, it was more like playing pin the tail on the donkey, blindfolded and spun in circles.

Considering my own near-death experience in the canoe, one thing was clear: Receiving a second chance at life is something that sticks with you. My only hope was to find the five who were rescued and see what had stuck with them.

My search for the five campers in the capsized sailboat was quickly becoming an obsession. Every night after work, I would head straight to my basement office and scour the Internet for information on places like Whitehead Island and Burleigh Hill, along with names like Stewart, Sherer, and Laylin. It didn't take long before I started hitting dead ends; however, I wasn't discouraged. This *Magnum P.I.* stuff was kind of fun.

I read the news article over and over, parsing and analyzing every word, looking for that combination of key words that might unlock the mystery that lay before me. My search seemed all or nothing. No mention was made about the rescue anywhere, yet there were too many hits that appeared on screen after typing the names of the kids. Every lead turned up another, then another, but eventually led to nowhere—or worse, in a circle. It felt like being lost somewhere off the Golden Road north of Baxter State Park. "Didn't we just go by that same stump an hour ago?"

I started expanding my searches to social networks and ancestry websites. Some might liken it to looking for a needle in a haystack. I wished it was that easy. At least with *that* scenario, you could narrow down your search to one haystack. However, I seemed to have count-less numbers of haystacks and no guarantee of a needle in any of them. I soon became an expert on knowing where *not* to look for the kids.

Then, after almost two weeks of searching, there on my computer screen was my first real possibility, Dr. Dan Granoff. He appeared to be about the right age, and I had his e-mail address. Now armed with that information, I needed to be careful.

With an e-mail you have one shot, if that. Spam filters are poised to send your letter to the bowels of the Internet and block you, never to be seen by the intended recipient. For two nights, I agonized over the precise wording. I needed to tell the story without being flagged as spam. Thankful to have the newspaper article to draw from, I was happy with my finished product.

HELLO

My name is Russell Lane, and I am writing on behalf of my father. He is 83 and was in the Coast Guard in the late 1950s. He talked about rescuing a group of kids off Whitehead Island, Maine. They were in a sailing school out of Boothbay Harbor, and they were coming back from Camden. By chance he looked out on the horizon and about a mile and half away he saw a capsized boat. Some of the group could barely hang onto the boat and it was a serious situation. They got all five people aboard and took them to the lighthouse where my mother gave them dry clothes and fed them. He had tucked away a newspa-per article about the incident.

As far as I can tell, my father did not get the recognition that he probably should have. He never really told much about it. He doesn't consider himself a hero, but he has always been one to me. I'm trying to contact the Coast Guard, my Congressmen, and anyone else who could help. The names of the rescued are in the paper. One of them was Daniel Granoff, age 14 years old. If this is not you, I apologize for taking any of your time. However, if you have any information that could help me, it would greatly be appreciated. I will include a copy of the newspaper article my Dad has kept for all these years. Thank you for your help.

Looking at the drab winter scene outside my window, I thought about how much time had been spent up to this point just to be able to send off one e-mail. Oh well, it's Maine and it's January. What else is there to do? My cursor hovered over the send button; I closed my eyes, said a little prayer, clicked the mouse and went to bed.

My hands trembled as I sat on the edge of the bed. It was 3 a.m.— too early to be awake for a Monday morning, or any morning, for that matter. With each word I read, my pulse quickened. I had woken only minutes before by an overwhelming desire to check my e-mail.

Trying to leave the room so as not to wake Heidi, my body, still half asleep, was struggling to move at my mind's command. It was an affliction I was becoming all too familiar with at this point in my life. Limb against limb pitted in a race for supremacy: curiosity versus consideration. Before my eyes opened, I reached for my iPad and swung my legs over the edge of the bed in an attempt to sneak out the door. My fingers found the e-mail before my feet found the floor. It was too late. Frozen on the side of the bed, I clicked on the e-mail delivered sometime in the night. He wrote me back. I couldn't believe Dan Granoff wrote me back!

Dear Mr. Lane... Thanks for contacting me... It brought back a lot of memories...

YES! It's him! It's him! An overwhelming child-like giddiness bubbled up inside my chest, a feeling that can only be compared to one other time in my life: stepping off the bus in second grade on that last day of school before summer vacation. Weekends lasted days, summers were an eternity, and that taste of freedom brought me to a pinnacle of giddiness not experienced since. That level of euphoria is a standard that can rarely be achieved again no matter how long you live, but finding Dr. Granoff was close!

Our boat was part of a group of sailboats from a sailing camp... We had been on an excursion to Camden and were sailing back to Boothbay Harbor, but because of a series of events, our boat was about 1-1/2 miles behind the other boats and out of sight.

Reading the letter in small chunks, I kept having to stop and wipe my eyes.

There were large waves. We had lost a can used for bailing, and eventually we took on so much water that the boat capsized. We also had lost several life preservers.

Oh my; I tried to wrap my head around their situation. All alone in a chaotic ocean, taunted by large waves and clinging to a sinking sailboat. It was a prize-winning recipe for disaster if I'd ever heard one.

Pete and Jeff positioned themselves on the bow, which was the only part of the boat above water. The other three of us were in the water holding onto the boat. The water was cold.

Much like gathering around a card table working on a puzzle, the newspaper article had laid the groundwork for completing the border. Now Dr. Granoff connected more pieces in the center. I was mesmerized.

I didn't note the amount of time we were in the water, but I did note that Leslie looked terrible, and I had doubts that she was going to survive. I was totally numb, and I thought it unlikely, given the late time of the afternoon and the large swells, that another boat would be near enough to see us anytime soon.

A sense of sadness brushed over me as I realized the true despair the young crew must have felt that afternoon. It sounded as though the circumstances had left them facing what no teenager should have to endure. At fifteen, how do you prepare yourself to watch your friends die and come to the realization that you might be next?

When your Dad's boat appeared, I thought it was a miracle.

Reading that line in the e-mail was akin to a sharp turn on a roller coaster. One line: despair, lowest of low; the next: elation.

Later, at the lighthouse, he said that his wife had been picking blue-berries on the shore and saw our boat but didn't realize anything was wrong until 30 minutes later when our boat hadn't changed position and our mast was not vertical. She contacted your father, who called for a Coast Guard boat because he wasn't confident that his small boat could safely reach us. He then decided to use the lobster boat to rescue us.

Blueberries? My mother? What else did my parents and the newspaper neglect to tell me?

...I do think our lives were very much in danger, and I am grateful beyond words to your mother for spotting us and to your father for rescuing us.

My emotions, barely kept in check to this point, must have come out in heavy sobs, as Heidi awoke from a sound sleep. The room was dark except for the glow of my iPad. Much like a lighthouse, it helped her navigate the ledges disguised as dirty clothes on the floor along the way. Within an instant, she was standing right in front of me.

"Are you okay?"

Like a teary-eyed hyperventilating toddler with runny nose and all, I couldn't catch my breath fast enough. You could see Heidi's emergency response training kick into gear. She continued her barrage of questions, "Can you speak? Are you choking?"

I shook my head yes, then no. I must have looked like a bobblehead.

Reaching out, she grabbed my wrist to check my pulse. "You are shaking." Finally noticing the iPad in my hand, she asked, "Are you checking your symptoms on Web MD?"

Getting my breath under control, I could finally answer. "I'm reading my e-mail."

She loosened her grip on my wrist and groaned a heavy sigh, releasing air and anxiety from deep within. "You're *what?*" Her tone had lost its concern and was troubling to me. I feared her next response. Would she let go of my wrist and position her fingers around my neck? There is a thin line between checking for a carotid pulse and choking off the blood supply to one's brain. I was sure everyone involved—from the ambulance crew to the coroner—would have been sympathetic to her plight. No one would have questioned her story. "I don't know what happened Officer, he got up in the middle of the night, stubbed his toe, and died of asphyxiation on the spot."

I was relieved when instead she laid one hand on top of the other, clutching at her heart, and collapsed on the bed next to me. Well, I shouldn't say relieved (poor choice of words), especially now, because it appeared she was the one having a heart attack.

"I'm so sorry. I didn't mean to wake you," I pleaded for forgiveness. She sighed another sigh. This one sounded a bit more relieved than miffed, so I knew she was softening.

"I got an e-mail from one of the kids that Dad rescued." It was obvious she wasn't as excited as I was. But it's hard going from dreamland to first responder to loving, supportive spouse in a matter of minutes in the middle of the night.

"Can you believe it? He wrote me back!" I continued fishing for a response that told me she was okay with me.

"I'm happy for you both," Heidi groaned as she rolled back into bed and disappeared. I knew all was forgiven when the voice from under the covers assured me our marriage still had a future. "You can tell me about it in the morning. I will be excited for you then, I promise."

I closed the cover on my iPad and the room went dark. Quietly, I stood, gained my balance, and snuck out of the room, something I should have done ten minutes earlier.

Making my way to the office in the basement, I brought up the e-mail on my desktop computer. Dr. Granoff went on to explain that he was never one to journal; however, he had made notes of the rescue. As I continued reading, I discovered why it was so difficult to find the other members of the crew.

My earlier suspicion that the newspaper reporter might have been more than a little confused on the facts was correct. Not only was it unclear whether the rescue happened on a Tuesday or a Wednesday, Dr. Granoff's letter confirmed that the article wasn't much better with names. Jeffrey Stewart was actually Jeffrey Stark, Susan Sherer was really Susan Cheever, and the reporter had been unsure how to spell Peter's last name. Dr. Granoff said that he was misidentified himself. His name was Dan and not Daniel as reported in the paper. Apparently, Leslie Lewis was the lone camper the paper had gotten right. They were batting .200—not a good batting average for a shortstop or a newspaper reporter.

Dr. Granoff finished his letter by saying that, over the years, he had not kept in contact with any of the members of the crew from that day. But after reading my e-mail, he searched for Susan Cheever. Evidently, she had been easy to find. Having her contact information, he forwarded her my letter. He concluded with, "Best wishes, Dan Granoff."

Settling back in my chair, I could feel myself smiling. It was a genuine expression that started on the inside and worked its way to the muscles in my face without any conscious effort on my part. Heaven knows there hadn't been a lot to smile about lately. This was one of the best kinds, a satisfied smile to myself that just felt good. But my work was far from over.

When I closed out my e-mail, the web pages I had been looking at the day before made their way to the front of the screen. As I clicked on each page, it was like following a trail of bread crumbs as I discovered more about Dr. Granoff's life. Each one brought me closer to understanding what the world had almost lost amongst the waves of Penobscot Bay so very long ago.

EAST BAY EXPRESS, March 2004

Fighting a Third World Menace—Big Pharma's greed didn't stop Children's Hospital's Dan Granoff from creating a meningitis vaccine for Africa's poor.

In 1999, three years after the worst epidemic of meningitis in history swept across sub-Saharan Africa and left 25,000 people dead, Dr. Dan Granoff decided it was time to try and combat the disease he'd spent his career studying and developing vaccines against.

SNOW ANGELS ON THE MOON

As I continued reading, I discovered more about the disease than I wanted to know. Affecting mostly infants, children, and young adults, it can sneak up on the healthiest among us. With flu-like symptoms, it quickly becomes merciless as a rash appears, to be followed by fingers and toes turning black like fruit dying on the vine. Almost nineteen percent of its victims who survive will have a limb amputated, suffer hearing loss, or receive permanent brain damage. Another ten to fifteen percent do not survive even with a vaccine.

It is rare in the U.S., with 2500 cases a year killing 300 people. Still it is devastating to the families of those afflicted, be it a healthy ten-year-old boy from Oakland or a UC Berkeley basketball player. Full of life one day and dead the next.

Apparently, as far back as the 1980s, the know-how to make a vaccine for Africa was there. However, the numbers to develop the vaccine weren't. There weren't enough people dying in the United States and not enough money in Africa, where the outbreaks occurred, for the drug companies to buy into it.

Enter Dr. Dan Granoff. He became the lone wolf to petition the World Health Organization about the need. He created a nonprofit organization to finance the development of the vaccine. Dr. Granoff then approached the Bill & Melinda Gates Foundation, which pledged $70 million toward the efforts.

As I scrolled through the pages on my screen, there seemed a gap in the timeline that followed. To my delight, I discovered that the good doctor's perseverance paid off with the next page.

PRESS RELEASE: OAKLAND, CA (May 14, 2014)

Dan Granoff, MD, of UCSF Benioff Children's Hospital Oakland's research arm CHORI, has been named the 2014 Maurice Hilleman/Merck Award Laureate by the American Society for Microbiology (ASM). Granoff is being recognized for his work on development of a vaccine against serogroup B meningococcus, which causes severe infections of the bloodstream (sepsis) and membranes covering the brain (meningitis). Granoff also played a central role in conceiving a project to develop an affordable serogroup A meningococcal conjugate vaccine for Africa, which has had enormous public health benefit.

Pausing, I let the words soak in. Yesterday, Dan Granoff was just a name on the Internet, a mere possibility on a page, a long shot clear across the country more than anything. But today, as I continued reading, the *maybe's* and the doubts were gone. This was really him!

"Granoff is greatly deserving of this award," says renowned physician Stanley Plotkin, who developed the vaccine for rubella. "He has made outstanding contributions to vaccine discovery and development, disease pathogenesis, and immune responses to vaccines, particularly meningococcal vaccines."

"We are extremely proud of the research directed by Dr. Granoff in developing vaccines to prevent meningococcal disease globally and locally," said Dr. Bertram Lubin, President & CEO of UCSF Benioff Children's Hospital Oakland. "His research will lead to prevention of thousands of deaths worldwide." (I would later find out that as of 2017, the vaccine has been given to more than 300 million people.)

As I finished reading the accolades for Dr. Granoff, it was still hard to believe that he and the "fourteen-year-old" who'd written me sometime during the night were one and the same. It was like his e-mail had traveled through time before *Dan the doctor* even existed. The intricate details he had provided fresh from his journal were told in the voice of a young camper. I was just happy to have found *Dan the kid*. Now I was looking forward to learning more about *Dan the man*. And, of course, with four more campers to find, this was only the beginning.

CHAPTER 6

A LITTLE MIFFED

Pointing my browser to Google, I typed in "Susan Cheever." As the screen started populating with hits, I felt my jaw muscles loosen, allowing it to drop once again. Dozens of articles appeared with pictures and a sidebar explaining who this Susan Cheever was. The morning was full of surprises! First an award-winning doctor and now a best-selling author?

Grabbing my phone, I swiped at the screen. I couldn't wait to share my discovery with my parents. The time in big white numbers stopped me before I tapped on the word Mom in my contacts. Whoa, way too early in the morning to make that call. I had already come close to causing one heart attack before breakfast; no sense in taking another chance by waking my parents out of a sound sleep.

Sipping my morning coffee, I was hoping the caffeine would start to do its thing. The early-morning excitement had me a bit scatterbrained. Why wouldn't it? With one e-mail, I was hit with an avalanche of information: new places to search, new names to investigate, and new directions to go.

Thankful to have made the connection with Dr. Granoff, I still couldn't help but feel a little miffed about the old newspaper clipping. How could one reporter get so much wrong in one article? They sure sent me on a wild goose chase...well, not just one, but several. No wonder I had trouble finding the kids. How do you get Sherer out of Cheever? Or Stewart from Stark? I could have been looking for these guys forever.

I decided this wouldn't be the morning for pointing blame. What good would it do? Besides, the job of newspaper reporting in the 1950s couldn't have been an easy one. No tape recorders. No Internet fact checks. The tools of the trade were simple: a sharp pencil that quickly turned dull jotting down notes as you listened to someone's story. The skills of a reporter were ones that demanded the ability to multitask. Not only did they need to be able to document the details without looking, their mind needed to process the information and be thinking of the next question. Putting myself in their shoes, I started understanding what a tough job they must have had and how much they needed to juggle. After all, there was enough correct information in the article to get me this far. Where would I be if there had been no newspaper story at all?

With Dr. Granoff's letter I had a clear direction. No, let me rephrase that: I had several clear directions to go, especially now that Dr. Granoff had provided hometowns along with the correct names. With the excitement of having so many leads, I wanted to turn everywhere at once.

Glancing up at my computer, I saw a picture of Susan smiling back at me. Dan, along with Google, had directed me to her website. That's funny: When had I become on a first-name basis with these two? Maybe it was because I had been looking for a bunch of kids from a summer camp and that's who I found.

As I clicked from page to page, Susan Cheever's life opened in snippets. American author. Prize-winning. Best-selling. Her subjects were literary heroes like Alcott, Hawthorne, and Thoreau. However, her writings didn't steer clear of difficult topics such as alcoholism and sexual addiction. This woman wasn't scared of tackling anything. Her father was John Cheever, a Pulitzer Prize–winning novelist. So writing must be in her nature, passed down through the blood. I didn't have a clue as to what it takes to receive a Pulitzer Prize. Just one more thing I needed to research.

Heidi came down the stairs to my office, drawing my attention away from the screen. She was all dressed and ready to go out the door. "Are you working today?" She knew the answer. It was just her way of getting me moving without bringing out the cattle prod. "You'll have to tell me more about your e-mail tonight. Pretty exciting stuff!" Spinning on her heels, she offered a fading, "Have a good..." as she ascended the stairs.

Assuming the last word was *day*, I tossed back, "Thanks, you too!" It was too late, she was gone.

Darn, it was Monday, wasn't it? Between a shower and breakfast, I managed to write Dr. Granoff back. I included pictures of my parents in their heyday on Whitehead Island. Who knew? They might trigger a few more memories. Even if that was the extent of Dan's recollection, it was still more than I had hoped for. Anything I learned from now on would be a bonus! I knew one thing, though: I needed to curb my enthusiasm and get to my day job. My mind was swirling and eager to start researching for new details, so doing anything other than Googling for information would prove to be the most difficult task of the morning.

The day couldn't go by fast enough for my liking. It didn't help that I felt the need to check my e-mail every few minutes, hoping for another letter from Dan and possibly a connection to Susan. Some would say my behavior was OCD. *Obsessive, compulsive, disorder.* Those were three words that didn't always go together where I was concerned. The first two I could relate to. But what I was feeling inside was not a disorder. It was a driving force that filled me with excitement just thinking about what might be uncovered. I couldn't wait to tell my parents the news. And wouldn't it be something if someday all those involved in the rescue could be reunited? But, as most dreamers do, I was getting way ahead of myself.

I decided against calling my parents on the phone and telling them about Dan and Susan. Things like that are best done in person. Besides, it would be interesting to see the reaction on their faces. Checking my e-mail one more time before leaving work, a letter appeared in my in-box. To my delight, it was from Susan Cheever! Earlier in the day, I'd been overcome with excitement, tearing into Dan's e-mail like a child opening a present on Christmas. The afternoon had me feeling a bit more under control, so I decided to take my time and slowly unwrap Susan's letter, savoring each syllable.

Dear Dan,

Oh, my goodness! I like this Susan Cheever lady already, even though I wasn't included in the greeting. Who starts letters anymore with *Dear So-and-so*? Her e-mail was not like a letter at all, but more like she was

SNOW ANGELS ON THE MOON

entering a room. *Seeing Dan, she ran to him in a long-overdue affirming greeting.* I stood over in the corner quietly considering it a sincere privilege to be included in their reunion e-mail after all these years.

...That afternoon is, of course, seared into my memory.

Seared, great choice of words. How do you live through such an event and not have it leave a mark? In her case, it most definitely did. Turning her attention to me, she continued.

Russ, I have no doubt that your parents saved our lives, and let me add that they were incredibly gentle and kind about the whole thing.

This woman was a writer. Surgically precise with her words, she didn't waste anyone's time with fluff.

We were idiots. The camp was negligent. Yet your father risked his life to save us, and I so clearly remember your mother's offering me a drawer full of dry clothes. She was tender and warm, which was just what I needed right then.

In a few short words, I saw a whole spectrum of emotions come through in Susan's letter. Endearment and acknowledgment. Disbelief and anger. Gratitude and warm reminiscing. Like my mother had offered her the gift of dry clothes with an open palm, Susan extended the same courtesy to me in the form of her private e-mail address and her phone number. Thanking Dan, she left the room. Or, I should say, ended her e-mail. Not only had I connected with Susan, I had received a lesson on how to write a letter. Luckily, that was the first of many lessons she would have in store for me.

While driving to my parents' that afternoon, I had a difficult time trying to convince myself to play it cool. It was all I could do not to go in with both barrels blazing, "Guess what I found!?!" No, it would be best to not let on that I knew anything at all. The first few minutes of the visit were spent in normal, polite discussion that could have been pasted into any other day's conversation. It should have been a clue that today wasn't a normal day when instead of asking Dad to turn down the TV, I asked him to turn it off. Surprisingly, he did!

42

"What did you two do today?" It was a dangerous open-ended question, but I knew what I was doing. I lay on the floor patiently playing with the dogs while my mother went on endlessly about where they had gone for lunch. Waiting for a lull in the conversation, I saw my opening and asked Dad how his lunch was. Now knowing I had their full attention and their willingness to talk, I moved from the floor to the chair between them. It was a great vantage point to take in the discussion along with any body language. When Dad finished with the praises of his Chinese food, I changed the topic of the conversation.

"So, Dad, what do you remember about the rescue on Whitehead Island?"

"Rescue?" A puzzled look came across his face.

I spoke louder, "On Whitehead."

"On where?"

"On Whitehead Island," I repeated, feeling a little like I was part of an Abbott and Costello comedy routine, "when you were in the Coast Guard."

"Oh...oh...Whitehead," my Dad repeated. "To tell you the truth, I don't remember too much about it."

We had been down this road before when his memory seemed to fail him or he just didn't want to talk. I needed to prime the pump a little more. "So, what were you doing when you spotted the capsized sailboat?" Out of the corner of my eye, I monitored my mother's reaction. But she sat quietly listening in her chair, with the two dogs sitting on top of her feet.

"I think I was playing horseshoes. Yes, that's it. Alan Calta was trying to beat me at horseshoes."

"So, did he?"

"Did he what?"

Fearing the thought of getting into another "who's on first" routine, I asked the complete question. "So, did Alan Calta beat you at horseshoes that day?"

"I don't think we finished."

"Why didn't you finish? Did you look up and see the sailboat?" I felt guilty asking him a question I already knew the answer to. I guess that's what investigators need to do to get to the truth.

He started rubbing his forehead as if hoping to massage out the answer. "I don't know; do you remember, Sandra?"

A grin came over my mother's face, as if she had been waiting all her life to be included in the conversation about the rescue. Although it wasn't the first time we had talked about this, it was the first time I'd heard her next statement.

"It was me; I saw the sailboat." She was beaming at her confession.

"I don't remember you ever telling me that," I offered. "So, what were you doing?" (Still holding my cards close to my chest in this game of "go fish.")

"I was down along the shore..." She stopped to take a breath.

It was at this point I realized I could never be a detective in an interrogation room playing good cop/bad cop. I couldn't stand it any longer. Finishing her sentence for her I added, "...and you were picking berries."

Her mouth dropped. "Did I ever tell you that?"

Our roles were reversed; now she was the one asking questions.

Without taking a breath and with not one stutter or stammer, I blurted out all I'd discovered early that morning in one long, condensed run-on sentence. "You were picking berries, and you were tender and warm, and I found two of the kids Dad rescued, and they both wrote me back!"

My parents looked at me in disbelief. I wasn't sure if they were looking at me that way because of what I had just told them or because I was spouting like a ten-year-old. At least I had their full attention. With one more deep breath, I continued, "One is a doctor—that's Dan—he lives in California; and one is a writer, she's S-S-Susan from New York C-C-City; and they both wanted me to tell you how much they appreciate you guys for rescuing them."

The room filled with silence, not an awkward silence, but an awestruck one, as I paused to let my words sink in. My father reached for the TV remote sitting on his lap (its usual resting place until he gets tired of the conversation). What happened next amazed me. He picked

44

up the remote and placed it on the shelf next to him without turning on the TV. I do believe in miracles! All three of us moved to the edge of our seats like a team in a huddle listening to the quarterback as I explained the details of the last twenty-four hours.

That afternoon's scene of discovery and conversation would repeat itself many times in my parents' living room over the next few months. Although not much can compare to leaving them on that first night, I saw a change come over my father that was long-lasting. Whenever I visited, he would reach for the TV remote and push the off button. His life was worth living again, and news about what I'd found out that day was more important than a rerun of *Walker, Texas Ranger.*

Over the next couple of days, Susan, Dan, and I became acquainted with one another as we traded e-mails about the rescue. Reading and rereading each letter, I latched onto every piece of information that could be devised into a search phrase. It was in one of those letters that Susan thought she remembered something about their boat captain. With that two-word clue, the mystery of Peter Laylin's whereabouts was on the brink of being solved.

CHAPTER 7

TWO WORDS

It was as if Susan's letter only contained two words, and they weren't Dear Russ (although I still appreciated her starting each letter with such sentiment). In print, it looked like this:

> *Dear Russ.... Thank you for reconnecting us! The "skipper" of the boat was a counselor at the camp, Pete Laylin. And, I think he was a student at Colby College.*

Inside my head I heard COLBY COLLEGE...COLLEGE...COLLEGE. It read like an announcement shouted from the mountaintops echoing down through the valley for all to hear. It was more than just two words; it was a place, a place right here in Maine and a fresh chance to launch another search for Peter Laylin. Previous efforts had taken me nowhere.

Armed with a new search phrase containing the name Peter Laylin *and* Colby College, I made a beeline for my browser. Typing away, I would soon see the whole world of Peter Laylin open before my eyes. Eagerly clicking the enter key, I watched my screen fill up with hits—NOT! It was quite evident that Colby College was not the magic key. It was as if their paths had never crossed. It seemed like such a great combination of key words that I even went as far as searching Facebook. No luck, no Peter Laylin. Of course, Peter's generation doesn't live and breathe Facebook like many college students do today. How did they live without it back in those days, anyway?

There I sat looking disappointedly at my computer screen with the power of the Internet at my fingertips and no place to go. Google, Bing, Yahoo, and yes, even Facebook, had failed me. It was at that point I knew I needed something more. I needed Geri Wotton.

SNOW ANGELS ON THE MOON

Back when I was growing up, every hometown, if it was lucky, had a newspaper. Mine was the *Lincoln County News*. And every little village in that hometown, if they were lucky, had a Geri Wotton. Each week, she would pen a column on the happenings of the little village of New Harbor. Some might say she was a gossip, but it wasn't a matter of gossiping at all; it was about catching up with your neighbors. It was important to know who visited whom on Sunday afternoon, who was home from college for the weekend, and who was in the hospital and needed a card. These were the days when life was simple. No one was in a hurry, and we all seemed to like it that way.

I wasn't much of a reader or a runner as a kid, but every Thursday after school, I would race my sister, Becky, to the mailbox. Grabbing the *Lincoln County News*, I would saunter up the driveway, thumbing through the pages until I found Geri Wotton's column. More than once, my mother met me at the door asking if I'd brought in the rest of the mail. Engrossed in my reading, I assured her there wasn't any more. Becky would arrive a few seconds later with a fistful of envelopes. Busted!

When I went away to college and then served in the Army, my mother made sure I had my own subscription to the *Lincoln County News*. Halfway around the world in South Korea, I couldn't wait for mail call. Huddled at the back of the deuce-and-a-half truck, the sergeant would call us out by last name.

"Lane!"

"Here, Sarge!" I would yell out. My letters would be passed hand over hand, making their way atop the sea of soldiers until delivered to me. Once inside our tent, which held our entire squad, I would sit on my cot and read Geri's column out loud. Of course, the thicker I poured on the Down East accent, the larger the crowd of Army buddies I would draw. It was a funny thing: When I talked "Mainer," I wouldn't stutter *uh-tall*. One young trooper from Arkansas, upon hearing my "foreign" accent and discovering I was from Maine, was puzzled. He couldn't imagine why I was in the *United States* Army. Chuckling, I told him I wasn't sure why I was, either.

One thing I did know, though: The further away from home I was,

48

the more that little hometown newspaper meant to me. By then, the news was almost two weeks old, but it didn't matter. It was my connection to home and the people I missed most. It was Facebook before there was a Facebook. It made me wonder, did Peter Laylin have a Geri Wotton in his life, as well? And if he did, where would I find them and their columns from sixty years ago?

The answer led me right back to where I'd started my search, the local newspaper. I bought a subscription to newspapers.com that promised access to hundreds of newspapers nationwide covering a period of almost 300 years. It all seemed too good to be true.

Right from the start, I knew I was in trouble. It was more than good; it was too good. I was hooked. My mind went everywhere once I discovered I had the ability to tap into hometown papers from across the country. Newspapers.com was the niche I was looking for. It allowed me to drill down to the basics of everyday life in hometown America—places and times that Google could only dream of reaching! Of course, it didn't have all the newspapers, but it still had a good cross-section of the country.

As important as it was to find Peter, it took a while the first night for me to type in his name and Colby College. I was off researching other tangents needing discovery. The site took me beyond the history books. This gave me a taste and feel of what it was like in hometowns across the country during the depression, the Kennedy assassination, and the landing on the moon. It took me to Africa and to my Great-Aunt Pauline's experiences during World War II. And yes, it even took me back to a picture of a slumber party my mother-in-law had attended in the 1950s. I went all over the world that first night—so many different snapshots of time, archived in newsprint.

After being sidetracked for half the night, I was back to my research on the rescue. At first, I couldn't find that Peter had a Geri Wotton in his life, but luckily, I found that Peter's friends sure did. The search became like trying to scale the side of a mountain. With each step up, you navigated through the journals of time hoping for another handhold to appear, but there were no guarantees. Fortunately, the next handhold was always there somewhere. Someone from Colby College

SNOW ANGELS ON THE MOON

had Peter as an usher at a wedding in western Massachusetts. That led to Winsted, Connecticut, to a wedding announcement in the 1980s with a groom, Mr. Peter Laylin, and his new wife, Sara Liberty-Laylin.

I soon learned to love the name Sara Liberty-Laylin. It sounded like someone I should have studied in U.S. History class alongside Betsy Ross or Florence Nightingale. As I continued my search, when Peter's name failed, Sara's cut through the clutter. She surfaced in Washington State, where she was a principal at a local Seattle school and on the town's Art Commission. Peter was busy writing letters to the editor about excessive noise levels of train whistles in his town. They sold their house in Washington and retired.

Just when I felt like I was getting close, the trail went cold. Would the name Liberty-Laylin fail me? I started searching the nooks and crannies of the Internet once again and there she was. Sara Liberty-Laylin in Tucson, Arizona. I was soon explaining my quest and trading e-mails with my new best friend, Angie from Sabino Canyon, where Sara was a volunteer.

Angie "happily" forwarded my e-mail to Sara, who then connected me to Peter. Within three days of finding Dan, I was reading a letter from Peter Laylin. Three kids in three days. I was batting a thousand and overjoyed with my progress.

Hello, Mr. Lane (Russ)—

Yes, I was the counselor and the "captain" of my crew of four campers whose eighteen-foot daysailer foundered off Whitehead Island. I well recall the incident, and would be happy to talk with you any time...

This Arizona must be quite a joyful place. First Angie was happy to forward my e-mail, and now Peter was happy to talk to me! I was smiling. Wait a minute, did he say "talk"?

It would be nice if I could have a copy of the article (whether it's from the New York Times or the Boothbay paper)—I could put it in my yet-to-be-assembled scrapbook! So, give me a call at your convenience and we can talk about this some more. My phone number is...

—Peter

TWO WORDS

Seeing Peter's phone number gave me an uneasy feeling. His gracious offer to talk was a kind one, and no matter how uncomfortable it made me, it needed to be done. I picked up the phone and dialed.

RING... Now he has my number on his caller ID. There is no turning back. *RING...* What if I need to leave a message? Sometimes that's worse than making the phone call. *RING...* Just when I was about to convince myself that I should abort the call, a voice on the other end broke the silence. "Hello?" My mouth froze in the open position. The voice repeated, "Hello?"

With a weak, crackling voice, I answered back, "Hello, this is Russ Lane. Is Puh...Puheter there?"

"Oh, hi, Russ...This is Peter. I was just going out the door. It sounds like we have a bad connection."

I get these "bad connections" an awful lot, I thought to myself. That's the beauty of a cell phone. I can always blame my failure to communicate on cell coverage. Oddly, I was relieved that Peter was going out the door and couldn't speak now. It got me off the hook. We could postpone the conversation to a more opportune time. I could feel the fight-versus-flight battle for logic in my head. One side of my brain thought that postponing the call was a great idea, while the other side had a reasonable argument. The hard part was over. I had gotten the introduction out of the way. If I hung up now, I'd have to do it all over again. But he was going out the door, and I didn't want to be a bother. My voice became stronger and more confident. "That's okay, we can talk another time."

"Nope, heard you loud and clear that time, the connection must have healed itself. I can talk for a few minutes."

Soon I was settled into the conversation, like relaxing into a comfy chair and talking to an old friend. Peter was easy to talk to. I was grateful for my ability to hold the phone in one hand and jot down notes with the other. There were some days when such a feat of dexterity for me ranks up there with doing cartwheels and walking a tightrope. Not gonna happen.

Peter said he had indeed been a student at Colby College and had heard through the school grapevine there was an opportunity to work

51

SNOW ANGELS ON THE MOON

at a sailing camp out of Boothbay. He was hired and became a counselor in 1957 and returned again in 1958.

Without warning, my pen stopped gliding across the page. It resisted as I applied more pressure, only carving indentations on the paper. Oh man, out of ink?!?!

Peter continued without any idea of the dilemma at the other end of the line. "In 1959... Couldn't work at Burleigh..."

With no other pen in sight, I started drawing big circles on the paper to possibly jump-start the flow of ink again. Meanwhile, to my dismay, I was only catching about every third word from Peter.

"...spent...summer...ROTC camp."

The attempt at CPR on the pen was futile. It was dead. I gently laid the pen down on the table, more so it couldn't be heard at the other end of the line and less out of respect for the deceased. I already had a few last fitting words compiled in my head for the eulogy: *Frigging pen!*

"...then after graduation from Colby in 1960, I started flight training and became a pilot in the Air Force."

Oh no, did I miss hearing about the rescue? My heart sank.

I was relieved when Peter explained that was the overview, and now here were his memories about the rescue. He acknowledged that he hadn't known much about sailing, coming from the Midwest. He went on to explain that their sailboat was not capsized as the article said. It was slowly taking on water as waves broke over the bow. Desperately, they continued to bail, but they just couldn't keep up. As they reached the open ocean, they tried turning about, but it was too late. The tiny sailboat settled in the stern, and the bow pointed skyward and stuck straight up out of the water. Not sure how long they were in the water, but he knew things weren't good. Leslie by far was the worst. And he started to think of his parents and how sorry he was that he would never be able to see them again. Just when all hope was lost, he looked up and saw an angel. It was a boat coming directly at them with spray shooting out from the bow like angel wings. Finishing his story, it was time for him to go. We agreed to keep in touch. The phone call was over, but I couldn't get the two-word visual out of my head. *Angel wings!*

52

TWO WORDS

Putting down the phone, I picked up the pen. Its failure from a few minutes before was forgotten. After all, it had served me well for months. I just couldn't deliver the eulogy born out of frustration. Tossing the pen in the trash, I delivered a heartfelt "Thank you for your faithful service." All was forgiven. However, it wasn't just about the pen. At that moment, I truly forgave the reporter who wrote the newspaper article on the rescue. I had walked in their shoes for only a few short minutes. As a reporter, I failed miserably, but as a son finding out about the kids his father had rescued, I was on the right track.

CHAPTER 8

FACING GOLIATH

As I continued looking for Leslie, I must say it was disappointing when all my local connections failed to produce any information. My initial thought that Lewis was a good Boothbay name was dashed, and I don't mean in the good Liberty-Laylin sort of way. Evidently, Leslie must be "from away."

As easy as it was to follow the trail of Sara Liberty-Laylin, it was becoming quite evident that seeking Leslie Lewis would be the complete opposite. Sara's name was one of a kind. The power of the dash connecting her two last names was undoubtedly an investigator's dream. Looking for Leslie, however, was like looking for Jane Doe. Her name was everywhere.

On second thought, I think Jane Doe would have been easier to find. Looking for her would rule out half the population right from the start, whereas the name Leslie could apply to either gender, like Pat. There were girl Leslie Lewises and guy Leslie Lewises. Google then decided to reverse roles and started asking me, "Are you sure you don't mean Lewis Leslie?" Come on, Google, I'm the one asking questions here!

However, Google was right. Both Lewis and Leslie could be either first or last names, which could only add to the confusion. Maybe I was just plain "spoilt." After all, Dan had handed me Susan's last name and whereabouts on a silver platter. Lucky for me on that, because the newspaper would still have me searching for the nonexistent Susan Sherer to this very day.

Sara's hyphenated name, on the other hand, had blazed a trail across the Internet for anyone to follow. It had been too easy up until now. You know what they say: "When the going gets tough, the tough

SNOW ANGELS ON THE MOON

get going." But I was feeling more tired than tough, and the only place I ended up going was to bed.

The next day, Susan came to my rescue. All week long, she had been peeling back layers of her memories and sharing them. She gave me my next clue concerning Leslie. Just like her hint about Peter, this was a two-word place. Susan remembered something about Leslie and a town on Long Island called Lake Success.

Was this a real place or was fate taunting me? How could one fail with a clue like Lake Success? I had tracked Leslie Lewises all around the country and as far away as France. There were dancers and doctors and college professors, but they were all too old, too young, or the wrong gender. Susan's clue now gave me hope.

Finding the local school system for Lake Success, I contacted the alumni office at Great Neck High School and discovered a Great Neck North and a Great Neck South. Something left over from the Civil War, I assumed. Both sides called a truce long enough to notify their members of my quest. I started getting suggestions of people to contact. However, they kept coming up empty, which wasn't bad, just more leads to be crossed off my list.

It didn't encourage me when someone mentioned, "You'd better hope Leslie didn't get married; she might not be a Lewis anymore." With that uplifting thought, I decided to take a day off from looking for Leslie.

We were deep in the dead of winter, and my body had already stopped responding well to the cold. I looked forward to hunkering down in my basement office (the "dungeon," as Heidi called it). It was warm and cozy with a good Internet connection. What more could a blossoming investigative reporter want out of life?

Sunday afternoon came quicker than expected, and I didn't feel any closer to finding Leslie or Jeffrey. Cabin fever had begun to set in, so I drove to my parents' house—in part for therapy—and to catch them up on my progress, which wasn't much. As usual, Andy and Oakie traded barks as they welcomed me at the door.

Causing quite a commotion, I sat down on the couch and apologized for it drowning out *Walker, Texas Ranger*. Again, I was amazed that Dad did the unthinkable and turned off the TV. Moving to the edge of his chair, he inquired, "So what have you been doing today?"

"I didn't mean for you to turn off the TV, Dad. You can turn it back on."

"No problem," he assured me. "I'd rather hear about your day."

"You want to hear about my day?" I chuckled out loud as if laughing in his face. However, I didn't mean to. It was just so uncharacteristic of him. I felt a bit ashamed of my reaction. Thankfully, it seemed to go unnoticed.

"Did you find out any more about the kids?" he asked.

"Not really. I am finding out there are a lot of Leslie Lewises in the world, but I haven't found the right one."

"You'll find her, I know you will. I have faith." Dad's words were sincere and infused confidence in me. I welcomed the encouragement.

Mother came into the room and sat down across from me. Since I had nothing much to offer by way of new information, I figured it wouldn't hurt to see if I could jostle any new memories.

"When did you first arrive at Whitehead Island?" I threw the question into the air between the two—like a jump ball in a basketball game—and waited for an answer. Dad lunged first and tapped it to my mother. "I think it was winter, wasn't it, Sandra?"

"It was," she acknowledged. "We just had Becky. She was almost two months old."

I quickly did the math in my head. "That brings you to Whitehead at the end of February or the first of March. Does that sound right?"

My mother confirmed my calculations with a nod. "Yes, that does."

My question had gotten the ball rolling. Like a tag team, they took turns adding to each other's story. As they spoke, the pictures I had seen weeks before in my parents' photo albums began to fall into place. They merged somewhere inside my head like a movie. Taking me back to 1958, I hung on their every word.

It seemed to my parents like they were being dropped off at the end of the earth that cold winter's day. The Coast Guard boat that had just brought them the hour's journey from Rockland pushed away chunks of ice as it made its way up against the tall granite dock. It was low

SNOW ANGELS ON THE MOON

tide, but then Dad said, "It was always low tide when you had to unload a boat." The only obstacle between them and the island was a dozen or so ice-covered metal rungs driven into the granite wall. Dad made several trips up the treacherous ladder with their belongings. Mother handed him the baby as she made her way up the ladder and stationed herself at the top. On his final trip, Dad cradled two-month-old Becky in one arm and negotiated the crooked iron rungs with the other.

With the new keeper and his family safely on the dock, the boat captain yelled up, "We're heading back to Rockland. Give us a call if you need anything." With that, they cast off the lines and made their way out through Mussel Ridge Channel.

Abandoned on the island without a boat, they suddenly felt very much alone. With my mother holding Becky tight against her chest to share her warmth, Dad grabbed what belongings he could carry. They set off for the other side of the island and the lighthouse they would call home for two years.

I was amazed at the story that played so vividly in my mind. Why hadn't I asked about this before? However, I was just happy to hear about it now.

They both paused for a moment searching for more memories.

Poking my head back into 2015, I interjected, "That must have been awful, to be stuck on the island without a boat." I left the statement out there and, like a turtle, pulled my head back into 1958, waiting for a comment from the future.

They continued.

After meeting up with the two other lightkeepers and their families, they learned that the Coast Guard base at Rockland had a difficult mission. Whitehead Light Station was one of many lighthouses they were responsible for along the Maine coast, and it was obvious their resources were spread far too thin. The crew at Whitehead felt guilty asking for transportation—or anything else, for that matter. Besides, if they ever did ask for something, they did not receive the quickest response. So, more often than not, they found themselves being transported to and from the island through the generosity of mainland lobsterman Bill Butman, who asked nothing in return.

Almost weekly, Dad petitioned the base commander for a boat, asking, "How can we be the Coast Guard when we don't have a boat?"

The commander always gave the same response: "You are a light-keeper now, Lane. You don't need a boat."

That was funny: It sure felt like they needed one, and Dad was positive that, if the commander was stationed on the island, he would have had a boat. Of course, in the back of my father's mind, he remembered being at the mercy of the ocean the day he lost his best friend in the Navy. Not wanting to ever feel that helpless again, he had no problem challenging those in authority.

After six months of being the squeaky wheel, in August Dad's persistence paid off, and Whitehead Light Station got their boat. It leaked a bit and the engine kept stalling, but at least now they had a boat.

In one instance, my mother went ashore for a doctor's appointment. The weather turned for the worse and Dad was alone with the baby for three days. He soon discovered that tending to a baby was far more challenging than tending to a lighthouse.

For people who didn't remember much, I was wowed by the details that came out that afternoon. A lull in the conversation proved to be more of an indication that Dad was tired.

Having unlocked more of my parents' past, I thanked them and headed back home. Rejuvenated from the visit, I went straight to the dungeon. I started going over my notes from the week, being sure to add my parents' memories from the afternoon. Dan and Susan had been keeping me updated on memories that surfaced, and I was finding out more about Burleigh Hill Sailing Camp and its director, Lester Rhoads. Having no luck with searching for Leslie in the past few days, I moved on to Jeffrey Stark.

The 1958 newspaper article incorrectly identified him as Jeffrey Stewart. It was Dan Granoff's journal that set me straight on the last name of Stark. Not a very common name, at least in my circles.

Thinking Jeffrey might go by his first and/or middle initials, like C.S. Lewis, I began looking for A Stark, B Stark, C Stark—no pun intended, but I found myself going Stark crazy—D Stark, E Stark...After all, there

59

are only twenty-six letters, so what was there to lose? F Stark. G Stark...
Jeffrey G. Stark appeared on the screen.

Clicking on the link brought me to an e-mail address at a law office.
I jumped at the chance to write to Mr. Stark. I modified the original text
that had worked in finding Dan and Peter and typed Dear Mr. Stark
on the heading. It was a little after 5 p.m. when I clicked on the send
button. Going upstairs, I turned on the TV and put the search to bed
for the night.

DING, DING.

It was only an hour and a half later when my phone had other ideas
about putting the search to bed. I swiped at the screen:

Re: Rescue on the Maine Coast from Jeffrey Stark

Probably me. Camp Annisquam?

– Sent from my iPhone

I felt my pulse quicken. Could this really be him? This can't be him!
What's Camp Annisquam? Maybe he was testing me. After all, I was
just a guy from somewhere on the Internet. Either that or he had spent
way too much of his childhood at summer camps on capsized sailboats.

Returning his e-mail, I typed in *Burleigh Hill Camp* and clicked send.
Within a few moments I received another reply.

Re: Rescue on the Maine Coast from Jeffrey Stark

Probably me. Burleigh Hill Camp?

– Sent from my iPhone.

BINGO! I felt my fist pump in the air! However, my thought process
kicked in and squelched my excitement. Burleigh Hill Camp with a
question mark? What does he mean by that? He did say it was probably him. So it had to be him, didn't it? I was more than a little confused.
Sending him the news article, I sat with my phone on my lap poised to
respond. It remained silent for the rest of the evening, which gave me
time to discover more about the life of Jeffrey G. Stark.

Delving into the website where I'd made my discovery, I was in awe
of Mr. Stark's career. Over the years, his accomplishments had been

FACING GOLIATH

impressive, serving as a Justice of the New York Supreme Court and being nominated by President Clinton to be a Judge of the United States Court of International Trade. He handled hundreds of cases, which included everything from defeating former Vice President Spiro T. Agnew in a lawsuit, to pro bono cases helping foster children. He'd spent his life fighting for justice.

Not only was I amazed by the masses his life had touched over the years, I was equally impressed by the difference he must have made in individual lives along the way. It was 1970 and a young artist was at odds with city officials in lower Manhattan. His neighborhood was earmarked for a stalled urban renewal project. As the buildings came down around him, the city attempted to drive the artist out by turning off his water. He ran hoses from other buildings until they were demolished around him. They then formed a bucket brigade carrying water in five-gallon pails from a nearby fire hydrant. For two years, he lived without water, refusing to give in to the bullying. Enter a talented young attorney working for an antipoverty organization. His name was Jeffrey G. Stark. Asking the city why his client had to move out before renewal plans were approved, he was told "because we (the city) say he has to and if you don't like it, take it to court." That young attorney did just that. Jeffrey won the case and water was reconnected where the tenant remained for over thirty years until 2003. The case brought national attention to the rights of citizens and brought hope for those Davids who were facing Goliaths everywhere. They say you can't fight city hall, but Jeffrey Stark did just that and won.

Placing my phone on the charger, it was time for bed. I must admit I was a little disappointed that Mr. Stark didn't get back to me that evening. But down deep I knew that *probably me* was *probably him* and I had faith that he would get back to me sometime. I was just hoping I could go to bed knowing I had found the fourth crew member of the sailboat *Debby*. Turning out the light, there was still a shadow of doubt.

CHAPTER 9

BOOTHBAY HISTORICAL

Over the next week, I contacted Jeffrey Stark twice more. Both times, he said the news article I kept resending wouldn't open. I tried sending it in a different format and was glad when he reported back that it worked. I was just happy for his persistence. That could only mean one thing. He had to be the right Jeffrey Stark, otherwise he would have told me to get lost by now. I had found number four!

Getting back to my research, I wondered if the local historical society in Boothbay had anything on Burleigh Hill Camp. Finding their contact information online, soon I was trading e-mails with local historian Barbara Rumsey. I was delighted to find that they had recently received some information on Burleigh Hill Camp. Timing is everything! Just a few months before, Barbara said, they would have had nothing to offer. This made me even more eager to visit Boothbay. Who was this Burleigh Hill benefactor? Until now, I thought I was the only one on the planet with Burleigh Hill Sailing Camp on the brain. After all, the camp had been closed for forty years. We set up a meeting for the upcoming weekend, and it couldn't get here fast enough.

On Saturday morning, I pulled into the bank parking lot across from the Boothbay Region Historical Society. The inch or two of snow that had fallen earlier in the morning was more of a nuisance than anything. If you are not used to the snow in Maine by January, you'd better be in Florida.

Arriving a little early for the appointment, I waited in the truck with the heater running. My body just doesn't behave well in the cold anymore. I blame it on old age, but down deep I know it is something more. It didn't take long for a car to pull into the driveway across the street, and a petite figure emerged from the vehicle and walked to the

SNOW ANGELS ON THE MOON

front door. Not wanting to rush right in, I waited for a few minutes to allow her time to open shop.

After finally going inside, I wished I'd waited a bit longer for the building to warm up. However, I wasn't complaining. As with most historical societies in Maine, I was pretty sure they were on a tight budget. I went from room to room in search of the person I assumed was Barbara Rumsey. The lights were turned on throughout the building, and I heard the heat coming on. I suspected it would be a while before I would even venture to take off my coat.

Looking around, I felt like a kid in a candy store. There were old pictures, maps, and nautical memorabilia on display everywhere. I could've easily forgotten my purpose and just browsed through the museum part of the building all day.

A voice from somewhere behind reminded me why I was there. "You must be Russ. I'm Barbara Rumsey."

Turning, I saw a slender figure of a woman with an outstretched hand. Shaking it, I thanked her for seeing me. Both still bundled in our winter coats, Barbara led me to the back office. I started to unzip my coat, but the little flapper on the zipper held itself tightly against my chest, refusing to cooperate. That should have been my first clue that my medicine was wearing off.

Offering me a chair, Barbara reached for a folder and opened it on the desk in front of me.

"If you had asked us a few months ago about Burleigh Hill, I would have had to turn you away. We had absolutely nothing on it. However, we recently had a donation from a guy down in Virginia, so we started a new Burleigh Hill folder. You are the first one to ask for it."

With a nod I thanked her and got right to work. It would have been easy to become bogged down by reading each piece of paper or looking at each picture; that wasn't my mission today. I thought my time was better spent making copies for future reference. Besides, I had no idea what I needed as part of my research or what would become relevant down the road. Turning over each page, I snapped away on my camera like James Bond capturing top-secret documents for the doomsday machine.

64

With each snapshot, I was formulating an overview of Burleigh Hill Camp. It looked like it would've been awesome to go to. My own youth had been spent lobstering with my dad, and there were days when that was fun. Still, it would've been interesting to try a couple of weeks of sailing, horseback riding, and waterskiing at a summer camp.

After an hour, I was satisfied that I had captured the entire folder with my camera. Then I started from the beginning once again, taking the time to examine each picture and reading each piece of paper.

All the while, Barbara worked on her own desk going through files and making phone calls. Every so often, we would talk across the table asking each other a question. Barbara took the business of preserving history seriously. In sizing up her demeanor, I wasn't surprised when she asked, "So, have you stuttered your whole life?"

My initial response (the response that never actually left my lips) was, "Only the part I have lived up until now." However, I vetoed that answer and elected to say, "Pretty much." I liked this lady. She was very much to the point in everything she did.

As I continued to go through the file, my movements slowed down. I was fumbling with the pages more than flipping through them. My right side was falling asleep and not wanting to listen to my brain. I excused myself and shuffled off to the truck. Looking down at my footprints in the snow, the impression I was leaving was not a good one. I was barely picking up my feet, and my toes were acting like little snowplows. My body was begging for medicine as my arms and legs started shutting down, refusing to move. Fifteen minutes later, I was back in the office sitting across from Barbara taking mental snapshots of each piece of paper once again. My body almost felt back to normal.

"Are you okay?" Barbara's eyes softened with concern.

"Oh, I'll be okay," I reassured her, talking more with my eyes than with my mouth. "Just needed to take my medicine." (Well, that was a wee bit too much information on my part.) Something told me the conversation wasn't over.

"Medicine? What for?" Barbara asked in a matter-of-fact sort of way. She had the act of interrogation down to an art form. Had she used these tactics during wartime to help lead the Allied Forces to victory?

SNOW ANGELS ON THE MOON

Perhaps she had worked in the LA homicide division and was an expert at eliciting confessions. Either way, I was helpless in her clutches. I could do nothing but surrender with my answer.

"I have Parkinson's Disease." The answer surprised me. The words slipped out of my mouth—a little too easily—words I normally guarded close to my chest. Then again, it was a question that was rarely asked. Of course, there have not been many Barbara Rumseys in my life. Somehow the conversation was not awkward; instead it was like talking with a longtime coworker about the weather. She asked questions, and I answered them. No big deal.

Time passed, and Barbara stopped what she was doing and waited until we made eye contact again. Being sure she had my full attention, she said, "Nothing stops you, does it." I could hear compassion in her question. In fact, it really wasn't a question at all. She said it like a statement. I felt very humbled.

Touched by her sentiment, a smile came across my face. "Oh, I don't know about that, Barbara, it seems like things stop me in my tracks every day. But we all have to deal with something."

"Ain't that the truth!" Being old-school, she emphasized the word *ain't* more in playfulness. Barbara, of all people, had to know what my English teacher used to preach: "*Ain't* ain't no word." But it was probably her way of putting her seal of approval on my last statement. Looking down at our desks, we each returned to our tasks.

After reviewing the folder for a third time, I knew I had wrung out as much information as my brain could store for one day. Besides, having copies to take home was a great backup in case someone hit delete on my memory someday. I closed the folder and offered it back to Barbara.

"Did you find what you're looking for?"

"I think I have. Thank you," I said, waiting to be excused.

"You asked about Lester's right-hand man, Bob Goodspeed, in one of your e-mails. Did you know he sometimes comes in here?"

"I did not know that."

"Do you want to speak to him?" Not waiting for a reply, she moved her telephone to the center of her desk.

My fear of the phone came out of the shadows. My heart began to pound. "That's okay; I don't want to bother him now. Maybe if you had his e-mail address, you could give me that."

She either didn't hear me or was too busy getting down to business. "Let's call him up right now," she said as she flipped through her Rolodex.

Within a minute, she was in a conversation with Bob, explaining who I was and what I was looking for. Paving my way, she handed me the phone with a reassuring glance that all would be okay. She did more than hand me the phone; she handed me her confidence. My conversation with Bob was a good one and concluded with a scheduled meeting at his house for the upcoming Tuesday.

Passing the phone back to Barbara, I felt a deep appreciation for this all-business, no-time-like-the-present, compassionate lady. We shook hands; I thanked her and walked to the door.

Back in my truck, I sighed a deep, satisfied sigh. It seemed Barbara helped me with a lot more than just providing information about Burleigh Hill Camp. The morning was more successful than I had hoped, and I was grateful for that.

Tuesday came quickly, and I was traveling back to Boothbay in bright sunshine. The bitter cold kept frosting up my windshield the entire ride. As I crossed the bridge onto Hodgdon Island, nothing looked familiar. Then again, I had only ventured over in that direction once as a small child with my parents for a Sunday afternoon ride.

Bob Goodspeed's house was easy to find. He welcomed me into his home, which overlooked what I assumed was the back channel between Barter's and Hodgdon Islands. He was inquisitive as to the purpose of my visit, so I cut to the chase and explained I was researching about the rescue of five teenagers from Burleigh Hill Camp in 1958.

Bob listened intently as I told the story. In a thoughtful gaze, he seemed to be searching his memory for a link. After a few moments, it was clear he had made no connection. Our conversation turned to more about him. Bob explained that he'd grown up in Boothbay and served in both the Army and the Navy until he returned home to work

SNOW ANGELS ON THE MOON

and eventually retired. He talked about his close association with Burleigh Hill Camp and its director, Lester Rhoads. Bob was a wealth of information and soon helped me understand why I hadn't found much about the early years of Lester Rhoads. (But that's a story for another chapter.)

Bob wasn't certain when he'd started working at Burleigh Hill, but he thought he was there for five years. The camp lasted four or eight weeks during summer, depending upon what the campers—or, more importantly, their parents—wanted.

For what he lacked in knowledge about the rescue, Bob more than made up for in his memories of Burleigh Hill Camp. He gave me details on everything from how the plumbing worked to yearly accounts of all his projects. At his age, eighty-seven, I can only hope that my mind would be as sharp. He kind of reminded me of my father, a hardworking man of the sea, trying to do the best for his family.

Bob continued to explain that in the early years of Burleigh Hill, camp concluded with a weeklong sailing excursion up the coast to Camden. He described the trips like this:

"First day of the trip, we went to Tenants Harbor, then on to Camden, where we spent three days." A large van loaded with sleeping bags, tents, and food would take the kids to Camden Hills State Park. After Camden, they sailed to Spruce Island off Stonington/Deer Isle and spent one night. Next morning, they would make their way back to Tenants Harbor and then on to Boothbay the following day.

Lester, the camp director, would never sail along on these trips; he would just show up in his car to check on things and run errands.

During one trip—they were on their way back from Camden to Tenants Harbor—the strong tide and wind was whipping up quite a chop. They were just going around Whitehead Island when the lead sailboat was having trouble. Bob was only a few hundred yards away with the other four boats following behind him.

He ran up alongside and pulled the crew aboard his boat. Fortunately, everyone was wearing a life jacket. He remembered towing the boat back behind the island, where other sailboats followed him in. The lightkeeper and his wife came down to check out all the commotion.

BOOTHBAY HISTORICAL

Bob told him everything was under control and asked if they could spend the night on the island. The keeper said they were welcome to sleep in the boathouse if they wanted to. They accepted the offer and in the morning set sail back to Boothbay.

I asked Bob if there were any other rescues of capsized boats or campers in the water. He assured me there were no other incidents while he was there. By that time, I had probably taxed him enough for one day, so I thanked him for his hospitality and was soon on my way back home.

CHAPTER 10

A GAME CHANGER

When I was young, it was a treat to accompany my father on road trips to the big city of Rockland for lobster trap supplies or boat parts. We'd ride down to the waterfront and wind our way through the maze of alleyways. I would immediately become lost. It was as if the buildings were all floating on top of the water and would randomly rearrange themselves with the rising and lowering of the tide. It was ever-changing; either that, or I was never clever enough to figure out the maze.

Rockland had a smell of its own. Dad said it smelled like money. It very well could have. I was never able to hold onto any long enough to compare the two. The Rockland smell from my childhood came from a combination of sources, like ingredients from a Marjorie Standish cookbook. (For you folks "from away," Marjorie was the Martha Stewart of Maine before there was a Martha Stewart.)

The recipe-for-money-smell seemed simple. In fact, you could figure it out for yourself by getting too close to one of its sources. The recipe goes something like this:

- Take one part trace of the briny, oily bilge of the fishing boats lined along the dock.
- Add a pinch of pungent from the fish processing plant from across the way. If my memory serves me right, that plant was originally instituted to keep up the aroma and keep down the tourist population. It did a good job while it lasted.
- And finally, one part sweetness of the deep-fat fryer exhaust fans blowing out from nearby restaurants on Main Street.

The scents would all rise out of their respective sources and meet somewhere in the air. The gentle harbor breeze would then swirl the odors into a nostril-delighting bouquet as it settled back down over the waterfront.

Rockland wasn't just a treat for the nose, but for the eye, as well. It was a busy place with always something to see. If I was really lucky, we would go way, way down to the end of the dock near the Coast Guard Station where I could get a glimpse of a cutter. In actuality, it probably wasn't a cutter at all. That was just my name for any boat with those slanted Coast Guard stripes painted down the side of the bow. I learned later that a cutter was the term used for any Coast Guard–commissioned ship that is sixty-five feet or more with accommodations and a permanently assigned crew. As a kid, even a rubber raft from the Coast Guard was exciting to see.

On one trip to Rockland, I remember announcing to Dad that I had made a decision. I was going to join the Coast Guard when I got old enough. Knowing that my dad had been a veteran, I didn't expect opposition.

"Oh, you don't want to do that, Son. They don't have any money. You're better off joining the Navy."

No money? I couldn't imagine it! How do they pay for all those Coast Guard cutters? It just didn't make sense! But after some thought, I realized he was probably right. The recipe for making that Rockland smell didn't include the odor from the Coast Guard. They didn't have a smell, so they must not have had any money.

It was on one of those trips to Rockland that I first heard the name David Gamage. As Dad often did, he was quizzing me during our ride. It was a big world out there, and he knew what was important to pass down to a son. "Okay, so you got a runner on first and third, two outs, you're the pitcher and a grounder comes to you. Where do you throw it?"

We were heading through the town of Thomaston when I blurted out my answer. "First base!"

"Correct!"

Dad suddenly took an unexpected hard right turn. I grabbed the dashboard so as not to roll across the seat and onto my father's lap. Little did I know there were these things called seat belts that were stuffed down the back of the seat. I am rather glad I didn't know about seat belts back then because I wouldn't have gotten the real-life example of Newton's third law of motion.

"Where are we going, Dad?" I asked, trying to get my bearings.

"First base is right! Good job. Okay, bases loaded, one out—"

"Dad?" I waited for him to look in my direction. "Where we going?"

"Spruce Head."

"What's there?"

"I need to see if we can find a guy named David Gamage. He helped me rescue those five kids in a sailboat. Remember me telling you about that?"

"Oh, yeah, I remember." Looking out my window, I was silent for a second or two to be sure *that* part of the conversation was over. Like son, like father, he was silent, too. Good, now back to something that really mattered. "Okay, Dad. Bases loaded, one out and what?"

Dad quizzed me all the way to Spruce Head until we drove onto the island. There he pointed out where this David guy lived. It looked like no one was home, so we passed on by. He told me to be on the lookout for any signs with the name Gamage on them. But we never had any luck that day.

I'm not certain how old I was or how many times we looked for David over the years, but somewhere along the way we stopped. However, one thing I never stopped looking for on those rides to Rockland was lunch. And, there was never any better lunch than a hot dog and a chocolate milk from Wasses Hot Dog Stand. It was a heavenly combination that wasn't just meant to go together; they should have been married.

I think it was junior high when I started to question society and the establishment as a whole. By then, I was almost a teenager, pretty much my own man. On one occasion, Dad pulled into Wasses and we got in line with the five or six people already there. Waiting was part of the experience. You'd always meet someone who knew someone you knew. You could tell the tourists from the natives, especially if the natives were fishermen. If the tourists were in front, they would tend not to turn back around, and if the tourists were in line behind us, they would give a three-foot gap in the line to the fishermen ahead of them. Dad always told me it was because of the smell, which I never quite understood. To me, the tourists didn't really smell that bad.

Anyway, we often found something we had in common with others in line to pass the time. There was no sense of urgency while you were waiting for a Wasses. It was a strange thing: The longer you waited, the better the hot dogs tasted. By the time we got to the window of that little plywood lunch wagon, our digestive juices weren't just flowing, they were gushing!

Like always, we ordered two apiece with everything (that means without ketchup, which should be illegal on hot dogs in Maine anyway, I might add). Dad grabbed two chocolate milks from the refrigerator on the side of the hot dog stand and handed one to me. It was no big deal—we were getting "the usual"—but to tell you the truth, I felt unusual that day. I knew it was time to be bold and try new things. Walking back to the refrigerator, I reached in and exchanged the chocolate milk for a Pepsi. Dad didn't look surprised. He knew the time was approaching when his son needed to step out on his own. But he also knew how a Wasses hot dog and chocolate milk transcended all stages of life.

"You won't like it," he warned.

I wasn't trying to be defiant as I tilted the bottle and placed it in the bottle opener, but it was a daring move. I pushed down, using the leverage to peel off the serrated-edged cap. Not only was that move life-changing, it became the longest lunch of my life. With every bite, that hot dog stuck in my throat like a lump of sadness. Washing it down with a half-empty bottle of Pepsi left me empty. One of life's big lessons was learned that day: It is okay to question the establishment, but if you are wrong, your taste buds may need to suffer the consequences.

Now, years later, even with a renewed interest in the rescue, it didn't occur to me to look for David Gamage. After all, he was an old man back then, so he had probably passed on. However, I thought a trip to Spruce Head and Rockland might spur more memories from my parents. With me now behind the wheel, it was up to me to choose where we would have lunch. With that as the main objective, I loaded Mom and Dad into my car and headed north. I took a hard right turn down a now-familiar road in Thomaston. No one had to grab the dashboard. The seat belts did their job.

"Okay, Dad...who played Marshal Dillon on *Gunsmoke*?"

"James Arness."

"Right you are. Good job. Who played Festus?"

"Geez... I know this one...don't tell me."

"I will give you a hint. It's the same name as one of Maine's governors."

Without hesitation, he slapped the dashboard with his hand like a contestant on *Family Feud* and blurted out, "Ken Curtis."

Dad answered a few more questions and then became silent. He seemed content to look out the window at the houses going by. Was he looking for any signs that said Gamage? I guess there is always a glimmer of hope. Maybe David has kids that still live here.

When we crossed over the bridge onto Spruce Head Island, Dad immediately came back to life. This was fertile ground for him when it came to his recollections. Riding by David's house, Dad mentioned something about him being a lightkeeper. Just like my dog, Baxter, upon hearing the word *treat*, my ears pointed to the sky, and I spun my head around to look at Dad. Lifting my foot off the gas, we coasted to a stop. Dad had my full attention.

"That's the first I've heard of that. So the old guy that helped you during the rescue, was he a lighthouse keeper?"

"Nope, his grandfather was, and that's his grandfather's house, the one we just passed."

Good thing I had stopped the car; my senses were on high alert. Up to this point, I'd assumed David was an old man at the time of the rescue. The newspaper article had said that the boat used during the rescue was owned by David.

"So how old was this guy that helped you?"

"I'm not sure."

"Whose boat was it?"

"I think it was his grandfather's."

SNOW ANGELS ON THE MOON

"But the paper said it was David's boat." I knew it when I said it. That darn paper had led me down the wrong path again.

The more we talked, the more I realized that our David had been a lot younger than I had thought. With this information, it was a whole new ballgame. I couldn't wait to get home and start searching, but I couldn't do that to my parents. They seemed to be enjoying the ride and they looked hungry.

The ride to Spruce Head had paid off. It made me wonder if a Wasses hot dog and chocolate milk was going to have the same result. As a budding investigative journalist, I owed it to myself and my stomach to find out.

CHAPTER 11

DOCK THE DAMN BOAT!

The best thing about growing up in a fishing family wasn't the fishing, it was the family. They say it takes a village to raise a child. Of course it helps if it is made up mostly of your relatives. Fortunately for me, mine was. I started going sternman on my father's lobster boat when I was about eight years old. After all, you can't waste your whole life being a kid. There were things you needed to pay for, like school clothes and baseball gloves.

The mornings that stand out the most were the ones where it was "so thick-a-fog, you couldn't cut through it with a knife." With dinner pail in hand, we would climb into Dad's truck and drive to the Pemaquid Fishermen's Co-op (we just called it "the co-op" for short). I loved watching Dad drive. His truck had four pedals on the floor and a couple of different levers sticking out of the column next to the steering wheel. And, of course, Dad only had two arms and two legs, so he was forever stepping on a different pedal and moving some lever somewhere. Driving looked fun, but a bit too complicated for me to ever learn. However, Dad assured me I would be more than clever enough when the time came, and he promised to teach me as soon as my feet could reach the pedals.

It seemed the nearer we got to the co-op, the thicker the fog would get and the slower we would creep along. It was always a gamble whether we could go haul our traps or not. But odds were, sooner or later, the fog would lift a bit and we could eventually find our way out of the harbor.

Driving down the hill to the co-op, there would already be four or five trucks in the parking lot. Before Dad even stopped, I would be out of the truck and on a dead run down to the dock. Sure enough, about halfway down the wharf there would be the gang waiting for the fog to lift. Those were the days before there was such a thing as GPS, so there was nothing to do but stand around and tell stories.

Standing in a circle, everyone would step back, widening it to make room for me. With a nod of their heads and a grin, everyone would greet me without interrupting the teller in mid-story. I remember the top of my head barely came waist high to most of them. But that didn't mean I didn't have a place in the circle. Everyone was welcomed. You could tell they were my family; they all looked the same. Their top half didn't match their bottom half. They all had spindly little legs and tree-trunk torsos. Their hands were swollen from the sea, and their forearms were as big as most men's thighs. They were my father, my uncles (Junior, Lonnie, and Al), with a few cousins thrown in for good measure. Most had the same last name as me, Lane. I once heard a joke about the Lane boys that was as much truth as it was humor. They say "You can always tell a Lane, but you can't tell 'em much."

One thing I do know, they could all tell a story. The pictures they painted in my head on those early mornings would run the gamut from awe-inspiring to gut-splitting. Stories were not the only thing passed down through the generations; the art of storytelling was, as well. I remember feeling kind of guilty while they were all waiting for the fog to lift, because I was praying for the opposite, hoping it would hug the coast all the closer so I could linger longer and listen to the stories. These storytelling pods replicated themselves on docks all along the coast of Maine on foggy days.

One such place was just across the bay in the town of South Bristol, which some folks consider to be the Gamage capital of Maine. They are a family rich in fishing and maritime history, building ships as early as the 1850s. Harvey Gamage left a lasting legacy constructing wooden minesweepers during World War II, and fishing boats and windjammers into the mid-1970s. Since the Gamages were still a local family, my hopes were pretty high that I might find a connection to the David Gamage who'd helped my father rescue those five campers. Like looking for Leslie, I started locally but soon had to branch out statewide and then went national. This is great if you happen to be starting a franchise or hoping to go viral on YouTube with your cat video. However, it's not very encouraging when you're looking for a needle in a haystack.

Just when I think I have this Internet thing figured out, I am reminded that it is a living, breathing entity, always changing. Don't ask me why, but I can search for the same name three nights in a row, and different people pop up each night. So I consistently searched for David, and consistently he wouldn't show. Then, to my surprise, one evening there he was, just as plain as day! Why hadn't he popped up before?

Either way, it didn't matter. What did matter was that there was no question in my mind that this was the right David Gamage. His Face-book page was a shrine to Whitehead Light Station. If it walks like a duck and talks like a duck...

Right away, I sent him a friend request, but of course, I was counting on David remembering the rescue and recognizing the name Russ Lane. There was a real possibility that Dad's name wouldn't mean a thing to him. The day of the rescue was the first time they had met and the last time they had seen each other. There was hardly any time to get acquainted; they had a job to do.

Having the same name as my father has always caused problems for me. We would get each other's mail or phone calls. After a lifetime of confusion, having the same name finally paid off! David accepted the request. As it turned out, he had always wondered what had happened to my father. We started exchanging information and pictures. Since David was still living in Maine, we arranged a visit at my parents' house for the following weekend.

On a cold Saturday morning in February, David traveled the two hours from the town of Jay to Bristol. As my parents greeted him at the door, it didn't seem at all like the reunion of two men who had briefly met one afternoon fifty-seven years before. They were more like two friends—no, something closer; like two brothers picking up where they had left off, as if the rescue had just happened yesterday.

David proved to be cut from the same cloth as Dad and my uncles. He would easily fit right in with the best of them down on the dock on those thick-a-fog mornings (although he was a bit too wiry to pass as a

SNOW ANGELS ON THE MOON

Lane). When it came to storytelling, he was a Van Gogh. I found myself wishing for the fog to come in thick in my parents' living room so he would have to stay around and tell more stories.

David was a gracious storyteller, a trait I wish others would acquire. He wouldn't monopolize the conversation but wait patiently for my dad to join in with his stories, as well. That makes a good storyteller great, to know when to speak and when to listen. I was in awe of David's keen sense of humor, his vivid recollections of the rescue, and his wide knowledge of the coast of Maine. Moreover, 1958 was not a distant memory to this man; it was yesterday.

In preparation for the reunion, I had created a little computer slide show complete with music and narration to spark both memories and conversation. The bigger purpose, however, was to put everything I had discovered thus far in one five-minute package to show on my parents' TV. David could then tell me if I'd gotten it right. He didn't miss a beat. Listening intently, he would stop me and fill in the gaps as they appeared on the screen. David wasn't bashful about speaking up and correcting my mistakes, and I was so grateful for his perspective.

That afternoon, it was more than apparent that the bond formed between Dad and David fifty-seven years ago was still rock-solid. They had performed like a well-oiled machine in a difficult situation, and after hearing David's story, I could understand why. David was only sixteen years old when he jumped aboard his grandfather's lobster boat and without hesitation volunteered for the mission. You couldn't have asked for a better person to be at the helm that day. He had more experience and knowledge of the ocean than someone twice his age. It was almost as if his whole life up to that point had been in preparation for this very purpose.

David had literally grown up in the Coast Guard. In fact, while he was off in Penobscot Bay helping rescue the kids, his father was in southern Maine rescuing another boat. His father, Weston Gamage, had made the Coast Guard a career. Whenever David visited him, he was expected to perform as part of the crew. If they trained, David trained. If they painted, David painted. He remembers learning an important lesson about following orders at the tender age of eleven

DOCK THE DAMN BOAT!

or so. His father had been trying to train some of the young "coasties" on docking the forty-foot rescue boat. They were just not getting it. David's father decided to show them that if his young son could do it, they could, and he directed his son to dock the boat. Thinking the others would give him a difficult time later on, David refused. In so many words, his father explained that one does not question an order from the captain of a boat, let alone your father. He repeated the order, a little more forcefully the second time: "I said, DOCK the damn boat!" Immediately, David took control of the helm. With expert precision, he navigated up alongside and kissed the dock with the forty-footer. The point was made to the crew, and David never questioned a captain's authority after that. Well, maybe not out loud, anyway.

Not only had David been immersed in the ways of boat handling and being part of a team, his early summers had been spent on Whitehead Island. It was there that he learned about the island and its waters from someone who knew more about it than any other living soul, his grandfather and longtime lightkeeper, Arthur Beal.

As the afternoon reunion was ending, I was all the more grateful for the ride to Spruce Head less than a month before. It was then I had discovered that David was just a teenager himself during the rescue and could still be around. And to think I had almost never gone looking for him. Right then and there, I decided to adopt David into the family as an uncle. You could tell he and my father didn't want the afternoon to be over, but David wanted to be home before dark. Who would have imagined an old salt like David living in a landlocked town like Jay, Maine? But I guess that is what happens when you go to the University of Maine and choose a career as an engineer for a pulp and paper company.

The two brave men finally shook hands and went their separate ways for a second time in their lives. Something told me this time it wouldn't take fifty-seven years for them to get back together again.

Watching David drive away, I started realizing how much I missed my uncles and how grateful I was for the tiny village that helped raise me.

CHAPTER 12

MOUNTING PILES

The next few weeks were spent trying to keep the mounting piles of information straight in my head. It seemed that every day I was adding new names to the list of Burleigh Hill campers and new pieces to the rescue story puzzle. It was all coming in so fast that I could feel myself getting bogged down with just answering my e-mails.

During David Gamage's visit, he had given us copies of old newspaper clippings along with stories that he had written for *Lighthouse Digest* magazine. It was through one of those articles that we found out my father had been recommended for a lifesaving medal. This was news to my parents, who had never heard of such a thing. Knowing Dad had never received a commendation, talk of a medal surprised me even more. Thus, another question for the Coast Guard.

Of course, through it all, I still needed to remain on the trail of Leslie Lewis. Dad saw to that. Whenever I visited him or we talked on the phone, it would be the first question he would ask. "Have you found Leslie?" It was getting to the point where I would answer the question before he had a chance to ask it. "Hi, Dad, no Leslie yet. How're things going?" It was just my way of saving us time and conversation, and saving Dad a little breath. We Mainers are a frugal bunch.

Speaking of saving time and conversation, the slide show I had shown David worked so well that I sent it out to the kids who were rescued. They started sending back their own input and corrections. It seems I had stumbled onto the most efficient way to communicate the story. Instead of writing long e-mails with questions that would never be answered to my satisfaction, the slide show served to gather more response and create a consensus. With a little more polish, I planned to show it to the Coast Guard, my senators, and anyone else

SNOW ANGELS ON THE MOON

who would watch it. Now it wasn't just Dad I was advocating for, but I wanted to see David Gamage and my mother receive the recognition they deserved.

In going over pictures to use in the slide show, one of the gems found in the archives of the Boothbay Region Historical Society took me in another direction. It was a picture of four kids in a sailboat. These would have been some of the campers who did make it to their destination of Tenants Harbor the day of the rescue. In posing for the picture, they looked like kids who could easily have been friends from my own childhood. The caption listed their names as Rick Rhoads, Mark Abeles, Tim Jerome, and my new favorite kid's name, Suki Gutman.

Two of them were already familiar to me: Rick Rhoads, who was the son of camp director Lester Rhoads, and Tim Jerome, a name first mentioned by Susan Cheever. She remembered Tim from camp but had lost track until years later. The two met up again in New York City. Tim had become an actor and had told her it was at Burleigh Hill where he discovered he had a knack for singing and playing the guitar.

With a quick Internet search, I was soon looking at a head shot of Tim Jerome. With the two pictures side by side, it was clear that Tim's facial features and infectious smile had not changed over the years. The bio said he was born in 1943, so it fit. He was a Tony-nominated actor on Broadway and had roles in feature films. Tim was easy to find. I didn't expect him to respond as quickly as he did. But like many things on this journey, the things I anticipated would happen rarely did, and vice versa. He contacted me almost immediately, commenting that he had the same group picture hanging on his wall.

The thought of being in touch with someone who might be able to give me a perspective from the other boats was exciting. Tim wanted more information about the incident to help jar his memory, but nothing shook loose. However, he did remember that he and Rick Rhoads had capsized earlier that summer during a race in Boothbay Harbor and had to be rescued by the camp powerboat.

Reading his e-mail was intriguing. I didn't just read it; I heard it. It was as if his lines were from Shakespeare. For some strange, unknown reason, as my eyes followed the words on the screen, I could hear a strong, rich voice that I envisioned to be Tim's (which, by the way, I had never heard before). I could imagine him up on stage, stepping forward to speak the part:

Reading the account, I began to feel the immensity of the running total of human experience. The memory of this incident started to re-emerge as if through a mist. I must say, though, that the incident was entirely peripheral to my own cruise experience. I wasn't on the boat and we'd get less-than-memorable updates; and the message was—they're fine and on their way back.

Tim apologized for not remembering the names of the counselors or the other campers and having nothing more to add to the story. He did, however, remember meeting up with Rick Rhoads while a grad student in New York, but they, too, had never kept in touch. I was thinking to myself how neat it would be if I could find Rick and reconnect them.

My sights were soon set on Rick Rhoads. Several sources told me that Rick had moved to Los Angeles. It didn't take too much effort to track him down. Rick's first e-mail said he remembered the incident and would help in any way he could to see that my father was recognized for his heroics. Finally, things were falling into place.

Then, without notice, my priorities changed. My father's health was beginning to concern us again. He was developing a cough and we feared a relapse of pneumonia. All his ailments seemed to be taking a toll. So many times in the past, Dad had bounced back from everything, from diabetes to cancer. He was a tough old bird, but we all knew someday we wouldn't be so lucky. Recently, I had seen such a remarkable turn in his demeanor and attitude toward living. Now that he had something to live for, it would be just like fickle fate to take it all away. But where fate might leave you doubtful, faith can bring you back to the side of hope. I stopped thinking negative thoughts and got the ball rolling.

I started making inquiries on how to best contact my senators and the Coast Guard. It was brought to my attention that a friend from high school had a niece who worked in Senator Susan Collins's office. I e-mailed my schoolmate, Debbie, and told her the situation. I included a link to the slide show. The next day, I received a call from Senator

SNOW ANGELS ON THE MOON

Collins's office. The ball indeed had started rolling. With the completion of a few forms, the Coast Guard review would begin.

Since discovering the kids my father had rescued, the thought of a reunion had been in the back of my mind. However, I never did entertain it to the point where I thought it could actually happen. Would these kids ever consider coming to Maine to meet with my parents? It was a lot to ask, but if I reached out first, it might be of some encouragement to them, as well.

As with most coincidences in this story, my son had moved to the West Coast the previous year. Historically, I can only go so long without seeing my kids, and I had never gone this long before. I couldn't stand it much longer. You know, I thought to myself, I could swing by San Francisco on the way to LA and take Dan Granoff to dinner. And while visiting my son in North Hollywood, I could possibly connect with Rick Rhoads in Los Angeles.

For every thought that led me to pursue a trip to the West Coast, there were as many that were against it. Heidi could not take the time off from work, and I was not sure how receptive Dan would be to a visit. After all, it is one thing to invite someone into your world, but quite another to insert yourself into theirs. But it wouldn't hurt to ask.

Checking in with my son, I was happy to learn that March was open on their calendar for a visit. Floating the idea to Heidi turned out just as I'd expected; she thought it would be great. With one more hurdle to go, I e-mailed the idea to Dan. He welcomed my visit and soon we firmed up the dates. My plane would arrive on a Thursday afternoon in time to have dinner with Dan. He offered to give me a walking tour of San Francisco the next day before I flew off to Burbank to meet up with my son.

The week before the trip was a busy one. After making finishing touches, I sent the slide show out to everyone for feedback. As I'd hoped would happen, Rick Rhoads reconnected with Tim Jerome and their reunion was planned. In fact, as a result of my research, other Burleigh Hill campers were finding one another after all these years. We weren't sure what was to become of my endeavor in finding recognition for my father, but one thing we did know—it was bringing people back together.

CHAPTER 13

GO WEST, YOUNG MAN

As the airplane began its takeoff roll, I reclined my seat in hopes of a nap before touching down at Newark. I was running a sleep deficit for the day. Earlier, when my alarm had gone off at 2:45 a.m., I was up and already dressed. The Portland Jetport website recommended arriving ninety minutes before my departure. I had my suspicions that 4:30 a.m. might be a tad too early. After I left my car in an all-but-abandoned parking lot, I walked into a ghost town of a terminal and those suspicions were confirmed. Traveling across the country to meet up with Dr. Dan Granoff was going to be a long day no matter how I sliced it. However, it couldn't be as bad as the last time I'd flown to the West Coast. That had been the longest day of my life, some thirty years ago.

Back then during takeoff, I wasn't thinking about reclining or catching up on my sleep. Sitting on the edge of my seat, I was looking out my window through tear-filled eyes. Gathering my last few glimpses of home, I tucked them away as memories for safekeeping. They would need to sustain me for the next twelve months. As we accelerated, the world I loved sped by faster and faster. My eyes were drawn to three figures standing at the fence on the side of the runway: my parents along with my young wife, Heidi, and she was holding our one-month-old baby daughter, Amanda. Their arms were stretched toward the sky waving goodbye. As the pilot pulled back on the yoke, the plane's landing gear parted ways with the ground and I could feel my heart break. It wasn't quick and clean, but a slow agonizing fracture with jagged edges that I was sure would never heal. As quickly as my family had come into view, with airspeed and altitude, they were gone, and I was on my way to Korea.

SNOW ANGELS ON THE MOON

The Army called it a hardship tour. They couldn't have picked a better name. Spending a year of your life away from the ones you love couldn't really be considered living. It was going to be tough on us all. We had experienced some form of separation before, Heidi and I, but it had been only a few hundred miles or so. No matter where I was, I could go outside at night and look up at the moon and think about Heidi. And there was always a chance she could be outside looking up at the same moon, thinking about me. There was some level of comfort there, that the moon would keep us connected, bouncing back "I love you's" to each other in the evening sky. But Korea would be different. We'd be looking at opposite ends of the universe. Separated not just by distance, but by time. Her day was my night. We had to endure an uncommon moon.

A voice suddenly came over the loudspeaker, pulling me back to 2015. "Please bring your seat backs and tray tables to the upright position in preparation for landing." It had been a smooth, uneventful flight so far. As we dropped into the darkness of a cloud, the plane shook as if the pilot had taken a quick turn down a gravelly washboard road. The lady next to me reached for her airsick bag. I was tempted to put my fingers in my ears and loudly sing out, "La-la-la-la!" With my eyes glued to the passing cloud, I tried to ignore what was happening next to me. I was hoping this wasn't an indication of how the rest of the trip would be.

Fortunately, it wasn't. The lady beside me survived her ordeal, and I did not follow her lead in playing monkey see, monkey do with an airsick bag. Changing planes in Newark was a breeze, and I got my nap in somewhere over the Midwest before landing in San Francisco. My thoughts turned to the adventure before me as we taxied to the gate. Three months earlier, Dr. Dan Granoff had not been on my radar. Now he seemed like an old friend, someone I had spent summer camp with. Though none of that had happened, in a strange way it *felt* like it did; and when Dan had answered my e-mail back in January, it had been life-changing for my aging and ailing father. The same man who thought his life was a failure and had no qualms most days about telling you he just wanted to die suddenly had a reason to live.

GO WEST, YOUNG MAN

Waiting to be the last one off the plane, I anticipated difficulty in getting up out of my seat. After sitting for so long, everyone is stiff. The only difference is that after a few moments of stretching, most of the other passengers come out of it. My Parkinson's, however, can hold me hostage anywhere from fifteen to forty-five minutes after taking my medicine. Until that point, my life is in slow motion, which still beats no motion at all. I grabbed my carry-on from the overhead compartment and shuffled past the flight attendant. Walking on my tiptoes up the jetway, I was glad no one was behind me to see the effect of what not having medicine in my system looks like. Then, upon breaking out into the terminal, I tried blending into the crowd. However, as people passed me by on both sides, I must have appeared like an old man holding up traffic on the Maine Turnpike, with my blinker unknowingly on. Though I tried to hold off on medication until the last minute, I knew I couldn't wait any longer. Finding a water fountain, I took my pills and set my sights on getting to my hotel. I was off like a herd of turtles. (Though unfortunately true, the visual makes me chuckle.)

Dan had provided good directions on how to catch a shared van to downtown San Francisco. By the time I checked into my room, the medicine was just kicking in. It was still a good three hours before I needed to meet Dan for dinner, and I was a little worried. Since I had just jumped a bunch of time zones, I was destined to run out of my allotted medicine for the day before running out of daylight. Although my feet wanted to walk, my brain convinced the rest of me to lie down for a nap and clear my head. The thought, though grand in theory, was not feasible. I was just too excited to sleep that afternoon. I was in the lobby way before Dan was scheduled to arrive. My pacing rivaled that of an expectant father. I nearly wore a groove into the floor between the back and front entrances of the hotel.

When Dan finally arrived, we greeted each other with a handshake. It was firm and welcoming. Tall and lanky, he had a wide smile. I thought it would be all I could do to hold back from giving my "old friend" from Burleigh Hill Sailing Camp a hug, but this wasn't quite the Dan I had envisioned. He wasn't the fourteen-year-old kid who had

SNOW ANGELS ON THE MOON

answered my e-mail a few months earlier. This gentleman was much more mature and distinguished-looking.

Dan had made reservations at an Italian restaurant up the street. In an effort to keep on schedule, he suggested we start walking and chat along the way. My short stride was no match for his long legs, but I kept up pretty well, in a jog. Soon we were being seated by the maître d', and I discovered this was a *real* Italian restaurant. No spaghetti and meatballs here. At least that's what I suspected. The menu was in Italian; I had no idea what to order. I told Dan it was all French to me and that I needed to rely on him to make a recommendation. Dan was obliging.

I had read and researched so much about this man and his accomplishments, but I wanted to know more. However, Dan had left the award-winning doctor/scientist at home for the evening. Instead, he came as a fourteen-year-old camper from Long Island. Over dinner, we discussed the people and stories I had unearthed. Dan developed a sparkle in his eye as the conversation seemed to ignite more memories.

The discussion turned to the journal Dan had written a few months after the rescue. During camp, he had wanted to be on Annie's crew. At first, remembering back, he thought Annie was a boat, but now he was thinking she had to have been a counselor. All he could provide was her first name. A challenging clue, but still a clue all the same.

Our dinner came, and the meal, though exquisite, got in the way of the conversation. However, that wasn't the only interruption. The long day's travel and the wearing off of my medicine was catching up with me. I soon found myself hung up on a word in mid-sentence. Stuck on the starting s sound, like a hissing snake, it felt like time stood still and all eyes from the surrounding tables rolled in my direction. Feeling myself spiral, I stopped trying to talk and took a breath. Now my voice was stuck in neutral. Silence. Not enough momentum to make it over the hurdle. So I sat there. Looking up at Dan, I saw compassion in his eyes. He waited patiently and reminded me there was no hurry. He understood it had been a long day, and we would have more time to visit tomorrow. The tension eased in my vocal cords; I could speak once again. He was right. I was tired, and we still had tomorrow.

90

GO WEST, YOUNG MAN

The next morning before leaving my room, I checked my pockets for all my essential gear. Glasses, check; my wallet, check; pills, check; phone, check—I was missing my younger days when I could just get up and go without having to worry about going through a checklist.

There was no need for my pacing to let off nervous energy in the lobby this morning. This time, I sat on the rock wall in front of the hotel and waited. Looking down at my dangling feet, I was happy to see my grunge-colored sneakers. I had come close to buying new ones for the trip, which would have been a horrible idea. Most certainly they would have invited blisters. My old sneakers had served me well at funerals, at work, and at running a 5K. They were time-tested and a perfect fit for the streets of San Francisco.

Dan appeared from around the corner with the same wide smile from the evening before, one that I envied. My smile has morphed into more of a smirk over the years. Dan explained the itinerary for the day, and soon he was setting the pace as we walked side by side toward the waterfront. His wide stride from the night before had shortened considerably, and he appeared more relaxed. I know I was. There was no need to race anywhere today. My walking tour of San Francisco would prove to be more of a leisurely marathon than a hundred-yard dash.

Our first stop was the waterfront for a wide panorama of San Francisco Bay. My eyes started at the Golden Gate Bridge and skipped across the water like a stone skimming past Alcatraz and the Bay Bridge, and coming to rest somewhere in the city skyline. The mystique of San Francisco beckoned me in every direction. My entire stay was scheduled to be a little over thirty hours. That was just enough time to whet my appetite for the Bay Area and to see my father through the eyes of a long-ago frightened fourteen-year-old facing insurmountable odds.

As we walked, Dan pointed out landmarks and explained certain sections of the city. Without warning, he would change gears after being reminded of something from his own childhood or a remembrance of the rescue and share it with me on the spot. As we strolled through Chinatown, Dan explained that while other kids his age had pictures of baseball players in their rooms, he had a picture of his childhood hero, Jonas Salk, who was known for developing the first

SNOW ANGELS ON THE MOON

vaccine against polio. It was that interest that steered Dan away from becoming part of his father's manufacturing business and led him to become a doctor and a scientist.

Zigzagging down Lombard Street (the crookedest street in the world), Dan told me that he almost missed the boat on the day of the rescue. He had walked a block to buy two lobster rolls and made it back to the dock just in time to be shuttled out to the sailboat *Debby*. Dan was sharing so many stories about the city and recollections of his childhood and the rescue, I was hoping I could keep it all straight.

He proved to be a top-notch tour guide as well as a kind and generous host. Only a couple of times throughout the day did his delightful smile turn to a frown of disapproval. Both times, he caught me reaching for my wallet to pay for lunch or admission to an attraction. He made it clear that such a thing would not be tolerated on this day.

Turning the corner, Dan became fourteen again. He explained what it was like to be back in Penobscot Bay taking on water with each wave over the bow. The next thing I knew, he was in full camp mode, walking down the streets of San Francisco. He sang the same sea chanteys that they had sung on the day of the rescue to keep up their courage.

Dan's phone rang. Stopping on the sidewalk, he apologized for needing to take the call. His tone changed, along with his language from English to Italian, like the flip of a switch. It sounded official in the textbook sort of way, not the emergency type. I waited quietly. Hanging up, he explained it was one of his grad students from Italy who was doing some important research. He chuckled, saying they tolerated his speaking Italian to them, but it did help to keep him somewhat fluent.

Before I knew it, we were back at the hotel and my time in San Francisco was coming to an end. Dan had to leave but he wanted to be sure I was all set on how to get back to the airport. I assured him I was good to go. Thankful for his hospitality, I ignored Dan's outstretched hand when it was time to say good-bye. Hugging him like the long-lost friend that he had become, we then parted ways on the sidewalk.

CHAPTER 14

BEST FRIENDS

California was certainly living up to its reputation of life in the fast lane. One minute I was in San Francisco with Dan and the next I was standing on the curb outside the terminal at Bob Hope Airport in Burbank. It had been a long day, but strangely I wasn't feeling it. Looking for my son, Drew, I peered through each windshield that paraded by. I wondered what the chances were of spotting a movie star. The odds had to be quite slim, given that it was ten o'clock on a Friday night. Everyone knows that's when all those swanky Hollywood parties are just getting started. Not to mention, the only celebrities I would recognize were probably all tucked in bed by now.

The familiar face I finally saw beat that of any famous ones I might have seen, hands down. Drew pulled over to the curb and climbed out of the driver's seat. We embraced. It had been a long time since I had seen my son. I didn't want to let go, so I hugged him until he had to push me away.

"Nice hug, Dad, but they will tow my car if I stay parked here any longer." Drew smiled, grabbed my suitcase, and tossed it in the trunk. Hearing his quick-witted remark reminded me how much I'd missed having him around. I climbed into the backseat as my son-in-law, Josh, turned around and offered a warm "Welcome to California!" It was good to see them both.

Drew lived just minutes from the airport, and in no time, we were sitting in their apartment catching up and trading stories. They shared their journey of driving cross-country to start their new life together. It had to be sometime after midnight when we finally called it a day, or a night, or whatever it was. Before turning off the lights, Drew reminded me that we could sleep in. It was nice knowing there was nowhere to

SNOW ANGELS ON THE MOON

be in the morning. I just hoped my mind would get the memo.

It didn't. The next time my eyes opened it was still dark and only 2 a.m. in Los Angeles. That meant 5 a.m. in Maine and time to wake up, but I couldn't give in to my body clock. Closing my eyes, I started my sure-fire way of falling asleep—counting my lobster traps.

One, two, three, four, five traps inside of Knowles Rocks. This was something my father had taught me. One, two, three, four, five traps between Beaver Island and John's Island for a total of ten. He advised me to count my traps before I went to sleep at night. He said it would make me rest easier knowing all my traps were accounted for. One, two, three, four, five around the ledges at Pemaquid Beach for a total of fifteen. I have never made it to the end without falling asleep first. Now, years later, I still count my traps to fall asleep. I hear some people count sheep. How bizarre is that? They must be sheep farmers.

This time when I woke up, it was just getting light out and I was wide awake. For three days, I had been waking up with the East Coast and going to bed with the West. I wasn't sure how long anyone could keep up this pace.

Reaching for my iPad, with lightning speed and one finger, I typed in "Remedy for jet lag."

Jet lag, medically referred to as desynchronosis and rarely as circadian dysrhythmia, is a physiological condition which results from alterations to the body's circadian rhythms resulting from rapid long-distance trans-meridian (east–west or west–east) travel on high-speed aircraft.

What website am I at, Google for rocket scientists? Are there two different Internets? One for Maine and one for the rest of the world? Google seems to be a lot simpler back home.

Without any hope of finding an answer that I could comprehend, I turned my attention to Drew and Josh's apartment. It was spacious and wonderfully decorated. The only other room in the apartment that was separated by a door, however, was the bathroom. It was huge, with dual walk-in closets and a separate offshoot for the commode and shower. The acoustics were astounding—like a Hollywood sound studio. It was the perfect spot to work from while my East Coast body clock let the west-coasters sleep in. Grabbing my backpack, I quietly tippy-toed into the bathroom and barricaded the door.

In preparing my workspace, I laid a towel out on the floor and sat down, propping myself up against the counter. There was a flurry of e-mails to answer. Highlighting the spam and hitting the delete button cut my workload in half. One name of interest popped out from the surviving messages: Alex from Senator Collins's office. She needed more paperwork filled out before the Coast Guard could search my dad's records. I forwarded the request to Heidi and asked her to handle it. She has always been a good sport when it comes to stuff like that.

My next e-mail was from Rick Rhoads, son of the Burleigh Hill camp director. I had written him from San Francisco to ask if he knew who this Annie was that Dan had mentioned in his journal. Rick came through with the answer: Annie's last name was Colclesser, from Erie, Pennsylvania. He indicated that she had been a good counselor and quite the sailor. Thanking him, I told him I was in Los Angeles visiting my son and would love to meet with him, if possible.

Excited to have a new name to search, I abandoned my e-mail, jumped back on the Internet, and became immersed in the search for Annie. Soon I was piecing together the story of a gentleman named Ralph Colclesser, Commodore of the Erie Yacht Club in the 1960s. Could this be Annie's father? Lost in my research, two hours came and went before I knew it.

With a knock at the door came a muffled, "Are you okay in there?"

Struggling to get up off the bathroom floor, I was hoping I wouldn't just fall back down into a heap. My body had stiffened up with my medicine routine thrown off-kilter, and I wasn't sure if I would ever get it back to normal.

Opening the door to find Drew standing there, I offered, "Oh, I'm okay, just in here taking care of some business," I smiled, adding, "I love your bathroom."

"Thanks, we're pretty darn proud of it," Drew sleepily smirked. We traded places in the doorway and for a brief second stood back-to-back like Alexander Hamilton and Aaron Burr. After walking off my required ten paces, I turned to find my dueling opponent, Drew, had already used the bathroom and was back in bed. Silently, I celebrated my win by forfeit.

Settling back to the couch, I continued my online search for all things Colclesser. By the time we left to go explore Hollywood, I had already put in a good day's work, finding out that Ralph was indeed Annie's father and I had discovered her married name.

The next four days were jam-packed. I was up early doing research and staying up late playing tourist. Drew and Josh had a well-planned itinerary that took me to all the places I wanted to see. Though this was my first trip to Hollywood, strangely, I was revisiting the places of my youth. Places I had first discovered with my dad on those rare occasions when he let me stay up late on school nights to watch TV with him. Now, some forty years later, I was visiting the same places for real with my own son. During that entire week, I felt every bit the VIP sitting in the backseat of Drew's car as he chauffeured me around.

One of our first stops was a shopping mall in Hollywood. I tried to act impressed, but my performance was far from worthy of an Oscar. When Drew pointed out the caviar vending machine over in the corner, I knew we weren't "in Kansas anymore." Who gets a hankering for caviar in a mall the way I do for a Snickers bar?

As we journeyed past the storefronts, we came to a staircase that took us up to the next level. "Okay, guys, I give up. What are we looking at?" I was clueless—not a first-time feeling for me, I might add.

Drew's next hint was a big one: "Picture flashbulbs going off as you walk the red carpet."

"You've got to be kidding me. Is this really where they have the Academy Awards? At a shopping mall?" Maybe the Hollywood lights and cameras were more about smoke and mirrors than I'd originally imagined.

Venturing outside, things became a bit more impressive. Off in the distance loomed the famed "Hollywood" sign. At Grauman's Chinese Theatre, I placed my hands where Marilyn Monroe had pressed hers into the cement. I found myself feeling sad, thinking of how her life had ended abruptly at her own hand. I knew Hollywood had made her a success, but it made me reflect on what role it had played in her demise.

From there we made our way to the sidewalk where Drew pointed my attention to the ground. We were on the Hollywood Walk of Fame, and I was standing directly on top of Robin Williams. I quickly jumped off to the side; it felt awkward and downright wrong to be stepping all over these people. Evidently, no one else felt that way. Others seemed satisfied to carelessly step wherever or on whomever they wanted. Maybe that's how you get somewhere in Hollywood, but not in Pemaquid. Walking suddenly became more of a chore and it wasn't because my medicine was wearing off. Not only did I have to worry about "step on a crack, break your mother's back," I now needed to dodge the stars lining the sidewalk. Don't the stars belong in the sky?

I began to think about some of the stars I would like to see. Not the sidewalk stars, but the living, breathing persons. One name came to mind: Michael J Fox. He was my wife's favorite actor...well, either him or Matthew Broderick. (I would argue that Marty McFly would be a better role model than Ferris Bueller any day.) But it wasn't Michael's acting ability that has made the more lasting impression on me; it is how he is acting in real life while facing a debilitating disease. He is a shining example to the world that you don't have to just survive with Parkinson's, you could thrive with it. Michael became an inspiration when I received my own diagnosis in 2006 at the age of forty-six.

Out of all the places we toured that week, the ones that stand out the most connected me to stories that were close to my heart. Places like the animal hospital where Drew works. As he shared his adventures in the operating room, it felt good as a father to see what type of man my little boy had become. Strong. Confident. Compassionate. He takes pride in helping those four-legged friends that have become so much a part of our families.

Continuing on our journey to film locations, we traveled to Long Beach and toured the *Queen Mary*. Standing on the bridge of the massive vessel, it was hard to imagine any storm big enough to ever cause it concern. And yet there was one. It had weathered the very same storm in the North Atlantic encountered by my father the day he and his best friend, Billy L'Heureux, were sent out to resecure the lifeboats.

Our next film location had us hiking into the hills where they made the TV show *M*A*S*H*. Surprisingly, as we broke out into the clearing, the adventures of Hawkeye Pierce didn't come to mind as vividly as my real-life adventures in Korea.

It was 1985, and walking across the flight line, I heard a wrench hit the pavement. It had been accidentally dropped from atop a Huey helicopter. I walked over, picked it up, and climbed up to hand it back to the crew chief. He thanked me. As I was about to leave, he asked, "Where are you from?"

"Maine," I replied.

"I thought I detected a hint of Down East accent." He smiled. "I'm from Milbridge."

"Really?" I stopped short, not uttering my next thought. With that accent, I would have guessed Paramus, New Jersey. He must have seen the question on my face.

"Okay, okay, you caught me," he immediately confessed, looking like a little boy with his hand in the cookie jar. "I grew up in Belleville, New Jersey, but I've always loved Maine. I went to college at Orono and lived in Milbridge for a while."

"Ahh, a transplant from New Jersey," I playfully criticized. Not being able to hold back my smile, I teased, "Well, nobody's perfect. Besides, you seem like a decent enough f-f-fellow."

Over the years, people seem to be put into our path to help us along the way. Don became that person for me. I never knew anyone who loved Maine more than he did. He lived it. He breathed it. We became the best of friends, playing cribbage late into the evening and telling the same *Bert and I* Maine stories. He brought "home" a little closer and made the unbearable bearable. I couldn't have imagined what my time would have been like in that godforsaken place without Don there to save me from my despair.

My trip to California was a success even though I never did meet the camp director's son, Rick Rhoads. Amazingly, visiting Hollywood triggered more memories about my own life than any movie or TV show. And the mornings spent online on Drew's bathroom floor paid dividends. As I was getting ready to leave, I received an e-mail from the sailboat captain I had been searching for.

Hi, I am Anne Colclesser Faust. I was at Burleigh Hill Camp in the summer of 1958.

My hope of finding more answers—and maybe Leslie, too—were renewed.

Buckling into my seat for the red-eye back to the East Coast, my thoughts went to my Army buddy Donnie again. We had stayed close over the years. Working his way up through the ranks, Donnie learned to fly helicopters and became a warrant officer. He had everything he wanted out of life: a beautiful wife, two precious children, and doing what he loved—flying.

Then one warm April day, I was outside raking November's leaves. It had been ten years since my time in Korea. Heidi appeared out of nowhere, handing me the cordless phone. It was Song Cha, Don's wife, and she was crying. In between her sobs, I pieced together the devastating news. There had been a midair collision during hellfire missile training in the night sky somewhere over New Mexico. Don, along with two others, did not survive the crash.

Seeing each taxiway light pass by my window, I was reminded of the twenty years that had passed since that heartbreaking phone call. Thinking of that day still saddens me. However, the sadness never lasts long. Any thought about my friend Don always ends in a chuckle. What better tribute can there be?

As our plane lined up on the runway readying for takeoff, for the first time in a long time, I felt scared—not of dying, but of dying and taking my untold story with me. As the jet engines roared to life, I closed my eyes, not as much to sleep as it was to pray.

CHAPTER 15

THE ROAD *LES* TRAVELED

They say commercial fishing is one of the most dangerous jobs in the world. If the ocean or ever-changing weather doesn't get you, there is a good chance the boredom and repetition will. You can only fill so many bait bags or band so many lobsters before the thrill is gone. Of course, there is always that one chance for excitement when a rogue lobster (usually the biggest one you've caught all day) sees an opening. When you least expect it, they can latch onto your finger with the full force of one of those gigantic claws that makes up a third of his body. This, let me tell you, can really wake you up.

While out on the lobster boat, Dad was forever telling me, "Watch what you're doing, Russie!" I would've been in one of my Walter Mitty moments, lost in my thoughts—playing first base at Fenway or on Safari in the wilds of Africa—when my dad's warning would stop me in my tracks (which was a good thing, because my next step might have been my last). In a matter of seconds, he pushed the trap overboard and raced to the next buoy. As he gunned the throttle, the rope connecting the trap to the buoy would fly past my feet on its way overboard. I could have easily stepped in the way, allowing it to wrap around my ankle and take me along for the ride. That's the bad thing about rope: It doesn't have a conscience.

For every time Dad warned me about being lost in my thoughts, I would catch myself daydreaming a dozen times more. Things happen quickly on the ocean. I can remember looking up from the bait barrel on a clear blue sky one minute and being lost in a blanket of fog the next.

One hot August afternoon, we were tending our traps in the middle of John's Bay. Feeling excited about our evening plans, I was trying to

SNOW ANGELS ON THE MOON

decide what I should get first at the Union Fair—fried dough or French fries with the vinegar sprinkled on top (such are the dilemmas of life when you're ten years old). Dad pulled the next trap up out of the water and opened its door to take out the lobsters. Lifting my head up out of the bait barrel, I spun around and grabbed the string to bait the trap. I broke my concentration and looked past the confines of the starboard side.

"Hey, where'd they come from?" I gasped.

Seemingly out of nowhere, we were surrounded by a gaggle of tiny sailboats. A few moments before, we had been the only boat in the ocean. Dad offered an explanation. "They're a sailing camp from Christmas Cove."

Like a swarm of bees hovering around a hive, the sailboats darted to and fro around their mother ship, a powerboat. It was constantly busy lending a hand to those in need. Every so often, the wind would catch a sail just right—or should I say *wrong*—and flip a boat to its side, throwing its occupants into the water.

The first time I saw it happen, I panicked. Yelling out to Dad, I pointed to the people in the water.

"We'll just stand by here out of the way for now," Dad advised, pulling lobsters out of the trap and carefully measuring each one.

Doesn't he care? This can't be *my* father deciding to stand by while someone might drown! We both watched as the powerboat made a beeline to the upset sailboat. They helped guide the kids in the proper way to right the vessel. Soon they were back to the business of sailing. The more experience crews wouldn't allow the boat to get in trouble, and if they did, they could right the vessel all by themselves.

Dad explained, "sometimes the last thing people need in life is someone barging in and trying to help, especially when you are just learning. You never know when you may be all alone and need to rescue yourself."

I think I understood what he meant. It was a teachable moment, not just for the kids in the sailboat, but for me as well. Besides, they looked like they were having fun. It was nice having company and

102

seeing my own kind. Dad didn't seem to mind sharing the ocean with them, either, even when they got between us and our next trap. He just patiently idled around them. They moved as a unit, keying in on the powerboat like their own little solar system. Then, as quickly as they had appeared, they vanished, and we had the ocean to ourselves once again. Little did I know that this would not be the only sailing camp to cross my path.

Lester Rhoads and Burleigh Hill Sailing Camp were synonymous. You can't really mention one without the other. The more I learned about Lester, the more it seemed as though someone should have already written a book about this guy. First of all, his name would make for a great title: "The Road Les Traveled: The Life and Times of Lester Rhoads." You can't make stuff like that up! Well, on second thought maybe you can, as I would later learn he had changed his last name from Rosenblum to Rhoads.

During my initial investigation of Lester, a 1964 *New York Times* article surfaced entitled "Sailing gets a vote as a top character builder." The article described Lester's philosophy and how sailing builds character more than football, baseball, or other sports in schools. He was frustrated with how many sports teach its participants to take advantage of the rules. Faking an injury to force a time-out became all too commonplace. In competitive sailing, however, racers are taught that if they hit a buoy while rounding the marker, it is up to them to disqualify themselves. Honesty and integrity. What a novel idea! Maybe someone should write a book about that, too.

Lester was a high school gym teacher with a booming voice and a tough, task-oriented approach. Some people didn't care for him, but the pro-Lesters far outnumbered the anti-Lesters. I likened him to a drill sergeant at boot camp. He had a loud voice because he needed one. How else can you be heard over a noisy crowd and screaming kids across a playing field?

Growing up, Lester was talented at sports. He played for the New York Yankees minor league teams and was heading for a promising

SNOW ANGELS ON THE MOON

baseball career. One day when he was playing for their Triple A farm team in Richmond, Virginia, Lester broke his arm running into a brick wall while trying to catch a fly ball. The injury crushed his hopes of becoming a professional baseball player.

During WW II, Lester served as an officer in the Army Air Corps, eventually earning the rank of major. His military career allowed him to connect with some interesting and influential people. He served guard duty with Clark Gable on the beach at Pensacola. As a member of Special Services, he escorted Marlene Dietrich on a tour along the North Atlantic. The Burleigh Hill Camp recreation hall was lined with pictures of Lester and well-known celebrities like Buddy Hackett and Betty Grable. Apparently, Lester wasn't bashful and would never miss an opportunity to market himself, his camp, and most of all his philosophy.

Lester did not come from wealth, so the early years at Burleigh Hill were lean ones. He knew it was important to continually make improvements, such as new cabins and equipment. With that as his basis, he questioned every expenditure. But if they needed it, they needed it.

Not only did he invest back into the infrastructure, he used what extra cash there was to invest back into the lives of the campers. He offered partial scholarships to kids who couldn't afford the tuition. Public school teachers didn't make much money in the late 1950s, so many of them ran summer camps to help make ends meet. The expense of running a summer camp 400 miles away in Maine had to have been a huge undertaking.

The age of the campers was between ten and sixteen. There were also slots for seventeen-year-olds, designated as counselors-in-train-ing. Then, once you were eighteen and in college, you could hire on as a counselor. The camp was made up of young people in all stages of growing up, from adolescence to adulthood. Lester was acutely aware of *that* fact. He would continually separate boyfriends from girl-friends. (This is what probably led to the camp becoming all male in the mid-1960s.)

THE ROAD *LES* TRAVELED

Lester opened the camp in 1955, and it lasted twenty years. Campers could attend for four or eight weeks. Primarily a sailing camp, it also offered activities such as swimming, waterskiing, baseball, tennis, and horseback riding. From time to time, there were more adventuresome activities like hiking Mount Katahdin and Mount Blue. The week-long sailing excursions to Camden were discontinued after the Whitehead incident. The unpredictable weather and the long-distance travel could have been a recipe for disaster and nearly did cost the lives of five campers. Such a calamity would have been devastating not just to Burleigh Hill, but to the entire camping industry that reached far beyond the Maine border.

Although Burleigh Hill was not a racing camp, Lester worked to get it certified as a yacht club. This enabled the campers, along with the counselors, to enter racing competitions sponsored by NAYRU (North American Yacht Racing Union), which is now known as US Sailing. Some Burleigh Hillers managed to rise to the occasion and come out on top of the competition.

Out of the thousands of kids he taught, some say you would be hard-pressed to find anyone who wasn't appreciative of Lester. Once a Burleigh Hiller, always a Burleigh Hiller. Former campers and staff members would come back to visit during the summer. Some would even stay around for a while. Lester would find chores for them to do, such as painting or other maintenance. There would be enough food to feed them and enough room to put them up for the night or the week. No one was ever turned away. How could they be? They were Burleigh Hillers through and through.

The bulk of the initial information I gathered about Burleigh Hill came from the Boothbay Region Historical Society, thanks to donated materials from one of the kids at camp, Mark Ganulin. Once I was provided his name, I couldn't wait to write and thank him for his donation.

Mark replied, explaining how he came to Burleigh Hill in the summers of 1963 and 1964:

He (Lester) was my junior high school gym teacher in NYC during the time I went to his camp. He offered partial scholarships to some of

105

the neighborhood kids in order to diversify those who attended. The two summers that I spent at Burleigh Hill were life-changing for me in many ways. I studied naval architecture at the University of Michigan and have worked for the Coast Guard for the past thirty years...

Someone else who was a wealth of information concerning Lester Rhoads and Burleigh Hill Camp was a gentleman named David Dembe. Starting out as a camper in 1960, he moved up through the ranks as counselor-in-training, then counselor, and eventually taught the mechanics of sailing. David became a fixture at the camp for fifteen years.

As time drew close to the camping season, Dave and Lester would meet on Friday evenings in Queens and drive all night until they arrived in Boothbay. They would spend the weekend readying the camp. Once Sunday night rolled around, they would begin the trek back to New York, arriving just in time for Lester to be at work and for David to be back in class at NYU Law School. Lester took David under his wing and became like a father figure, which is a term I heard from others concerning Lester as well.

David was everything that a counselor should be. He was intelligent, funny, and friendly with everybody. Campers were drawn to him. David was also a good sailor, and was on the crew when Lester's son, Rick, won the Prince of Wales Bowl in 1969. Lester was so impressed by David's abilities that, as a faculty member at Kingsborough Community College, he convinced David to come teach the mechanics of sailing where they sailed off Coney Island.

One of the unintended happy byproducts of my research was being able to reconnect a number of campers. Such was the case of Mark Ganulin and his camp counselor, David Dembe. Now, years after attending camp, the student influenced the teacher, as David followed Mark's lead in donating materials he had collected from Burleigh Hill Camp to the Boothbay Region Historical Society.

Despite his vast connection with Lester, David had never heard about the Mussel Ridge incident and the rescue off Whitehead Island. Lester probably thought it best to never speak of such things. Instead, learn from the experience and carry on.

THE ROAD *LES* TRAVELED

Considering the thousands of young people that Lester taught over the years, combined with so many that reached back to thank him later in life, and it is clear to see that his is a legacy that carries on in the lives of Burleigh Hillers everywhere to this day.

CHAPTER 16

A WONDERFUL GIFT

If you have ever spent any time in Maine, you understand that breaking up the year into four equal quarters just doesn't work. We have different seasons than the rest of the world. **Winter**, the longest season of the year, starts whenever you don your long underwear. Come April, you hope to be headfirst into **mud** season. That's when the long underwear can find its way back to the lower bureau drawer. If you're lucky, **spring** arrives the first of May and lasts until Memorial Day, which is the official start of **tourist** season. **Summer** is by far the stubbornest, making its appearance only when it's darn good and ready, if at all. **Fall** sets in hard after the first week of August on those crisp, chilly mornings when vacationers are low on cash and we natives are running a deficit on patience. **Holiday** season starts the day after Labor Day. That is when we get our best present of all: We begin to get the State of Maine back to ourselves. The holiday season then blends into **deer** season, with the uncontrollable urge to wear blaze orange. Once your freezer is full of venison, **winter** is upon us once again and we start right back around.

Somewhere between mud season and spring, the warmer weather starts to draw the snowbirds back up from the sunny south. Annie, the camp counselor and boat captain I'd located just the month before, was also in her migration from Florida to Upstate New York. She promised to look for Burleigh Hill photographs that she had stashed away as soon as she was settled back at home. Annie proved to be a woman of her word. According to her e-mail, her mission sent her to the far reaches of her house, places that had gone undisturbed for years. Her efforts paid off big-time when pictures began showing up on my computer.

SNOW ANGELS ON THE MOON

As I opened each attachment, Burleigh Hill Camp came to life. There were pictures of the five ARROW-class sailboats, the mansion where the girls bunked, and the camp bus that kept everyone on the go. What intrigued me most was the group picture of the campers on the porch of the mansion. They all looked like they could be from my own childhood years. Within minutes, I had the pictures sent back out across the country to the other "kids."

Soon a consensus developed that the photo was from the wrong year, as Susan, Dan, and Jeff were nowhere to be found. It had to be 1957, the summer *before* the rescue. Thanking Annie, I was grateful for her hard work and contribution to the cause. She said not to give up on her yet—she would keep looking. Just about a week later, more pictures started to show up in my in-box. I could see why everyone wanted to sail on Annie's boat. She wasn't one to give up easily.

I'm not certain whether she had a flair for the dramatic or it just worked out that way, but the last picture she sent was the one we were all looking for. It was a group shot of Burleigh Hillers from the summer of 1958. With everyone's help, we started identifying the faces. Annie really had given us all a wonderful gift.

Meanwhile, in San Francisco, Dan decided to plan a visit to Maine. A date was set for May. After a little coaxing, he convinced Susan Cheever to come along, too. My parents were delighted.

Lying in bed the night before the reunion was like those never-ending nights I'd spent as a child on Christmas Eve. I was too excited to close my eyes, let alone entertain the thought of sleeping. Of course, Christmas Eve had a pressure all its own. My mother would put me to bed with a stern warning: "Santa can't come unless you go to sleep." Sure, I thought to myself, put the entire burden of whether we get any presents or not on me. My sister, Becky, would be devastated. Mercifully, sleep did come those nights and so did Santa.

The night before the reunion, it was safe to say that even if I didn't get to sleep, Susan and Dan would still find their way to Maine. Their plans were set. Dan and his friend Jessica were traveling from New Hampshire after first visiting his aunt. Susan was flying into Portland

110

A WONDERFUL GIFT

around noon and renting a car. I was to meet them at the Newcastle Inn so they could follow me to my parents'. Before that could happen, somehow, I had to get to sleep. I closed my eyes and started counting. One, two, three, four, five traps inside of Knowles Rocks for a total of five…One, two…Zzzz.

If I thought that evening was long, the next morning dragged even more. I knew I shouldn't be wishing my life away, but the afternoon just couldn't get here fast enough. Every clock that came into my line of sight needed either batteries or winding. The hands of time were standing still.

Then, thankfully, the time came to meet up with the "kids." Arriving at the Newcastle Inn, I was greeted at the door by the owner. Surprisingly, she knew my name and started asking me questions about my father and the rescue. Obviously, Dan or Susan must have filled her in on some of the story. Dan appeared at the doorway as I was in mid-sentence. Cutting my answer short, I turned to Dan and we welcomed each other with a handshake that morphed naturally into an embrace. Turning to his friend, he introduced Jessica. Her warm greeting and praise for my endeavors in making the reunion happen left me in search of words. I managed to eke out a whispered, "Thank you." After all, *they* had been the ones who had traveled all this way and deserved the praise. Having just returned from a walk, they explained they needed to run up to their rooms for a bit before they could go.

Left alone, I began to explore the inn. Hearing footsteps, I turned to see Susan coming down the stairs. She looked just like all her pictures on the Internet. Each step she took was done in a graceful, deliberate manner. There was something about this lady that seemed special. But at that point, I just couldn't put my finger on it. I surprised myself when I heard my voice asking Susan for a hug. Reaching out, she honored my request, and I felt a lump appear in my throat. I couldn't believe it. The reunion with my parents was really going to happen.

As we readied to leave, Susan decided to ride along with me while Dan and Jessica followed in their car. It all seemed so dreamlike as I drove through Scotty chatting away with Susan Cheever. Before the rescue, the only thing I was familiar with concerning her last name

111

was the *Seinfeld* episode entitled "The Cheever Letters." For a guy who wanted to be a writer, I sure didn't know much about the literary world. In researching Susan and her father, I found he had graced the covers of *Newsweek* and *Time* while she shied away from a writing career to become an English teacher. However, she soon took a job as a newspaper reporter and within five years found herself as an editor at *Newsweek* and writing her first book. Susan, now having authored fifteen books, had me somewhere between starstruck and in awe of her writing abilities.

Pulling into my parents' driveway, I felt a twinge of disappointment. Everyone was waiting inside to meet Dan and Susan, everyone except David Gamage. Unfortunately, he had come down with a cold. There was my sister, Becky (barely eight months old at the time of the rescue), my mom and dad, and Heidi, who was armed with a video camera.

As I walked toward the house, Susan went off in the other direction. Had I scared her away? Note to self: I really need to work on my people skills. I was relieved when I saw her stop to help Dan get something out of the trunk. I waited for the three of them to catch up, then we walked up the wheelchair ramp leading to my parents' home. Opening the sliding glass door, I began making introductions, but that proved unnecessary. Everyone seemed to know who everyone else was, and the ones who didn't introduced themselves.

My mother was the first to meet us at the door. Dad hung back. Mother reached out to Susan and they embraced. I thought they would never let go. Who could blame them after fifty-seven years? Finally they released their grip on one another, and my mother moved on to Dan. "I gotta have a hug!" she exclaimed. I think Dan needed one, too, as they leaned toward each other.

Looking up and seeing my father, Susan raced across the room with an outstretched arm. It was like she was reliving the moment, as she once again felt the arms that had pulled her out of the water so many years ago. Her sparkling eyes studied his familiar face. "You look just the same," she offered.

Reaching out with his hand, Dad patted her on the head like he was comforting a little girl. It was a tender moment that brought that pesky lump back to my throat. Susan moved off to the side as Dan followed close behind. He and Dad exchanged greetings with a handshake. Dad appeared to be glowing with a smile I hadn't seen come over his face in a very long time, if ever.

As we migrated to the living room, everyone started talking at once. There was excitement in the air. None of us had noticed during the first few moments of the reunion that Dan and Susan had come bearing gifts. They brought blankets to replace the ones they had been given to keep warm back in 1958. The kind gesture touched my parents' hearts deeply. It was the perfect opportunity for us to give them the gift bags we had prepared for them. They consisted of the group photo of the campers, a Burleigh Hill Sailing Camp hat (made up special), and a tasty Maine treat—lobster-shaped lollipops. The reunion really was like Christmas.

Soon all the commotion calmed down and the sidebar conversations ceased. No one wanted to miss anything. We sat in a circle taking turns lobbing out questions. Everyone had an answer or recollection to share. One question might yield four or five perspectives from around the room.

Susan confided that she'd had a hard time sleeping for a week in January after being contacted about the rescue. Reliving the memories had brought back feelings that should have been dealt with shortly after it happened. Dan acknowledged that he'd experienced the same thing. The incident had been buried by the camp and not talked about much by their parents. The kids had been left on their own to find a way to cope with the experience. All they could do was follow the example set by the camp and bury it as deep as they could and try to forget.

The entire afternoon was mostly spent in laughter, fact-gathering, and getting to know each other. Conversation ranged to far-reaching subjects. We learned that Susan's grandfather had worked with Alexander Graham Bell, and that he was the Watson of "Watson, come here. I want to see you." And Dan told of his experience of two other near-drownings, one off the coast of Hawaii and another while whitewater rafting in California.

SNOW ANGELS ON THE MOON

Someone asked Dad if anyone had ever reached out to thank him. He did remember there had been a letter from one of the parents and their daughter. But it was long gone. Susan said it could very well have been from her father. He was always a big letter writer and it certainly sounded like something he would do.

The afternoon raced by and it was almost time for dinner. We had made reservations to continue the discussion at King Eider's Pub, a local restaurant back in Scotty. Unfortunately, Dad had been fighting a cold, so he thought it best to stay home and rest. He was okay with the decision because everyone promised to come back tomorrow. Just as the afternoon session was breaking up, I received an e-mail from David Gamage. His illness appeared to be the 24-hour variety. He was feeling better and wanted to make the two-hour trip down from Western Maine tomorrow. There was a cheer from the crowd in the living room as I made the announcement.

The electricity from the afternoon continued through dinner and into the night. There was no such thing as a lull in the conversation. There were just too many questions. Not wanting the day to end, we followed Susan, Jessica, and Dan back to the Newcastle Inn, where we had a cup of tea and kept the discussion going.

As Jessica and Dan excused themselves for the evening, the topic turned to writing. Susan was a great communicator and teacher. She explained the process of writing a book and getting it published. She was witty and informative all at the same time. Then it hit me, that thing I couldn't put my finger on about Susan earlier. Her smile combined with her easygoing personality enabled her to fit in where she was planted. In turn, she made everyone feel accepted and at ease. It was something I could only describe as the Cheever Charm.

Susan returned the next morning to spend more time getting to know my parents and their story. Dan and Jessica were off to tour the Coastal Maine Botanical Gardens in Boothbay. That afternoon, we found ourselves all back in a circle in my parents' living room telling stories. It was reminiscent of those foggy mornings on the dock with my uncles. This was an encore of yesterday, but with the gladdening

A WONDERFUL GIFT

addition of David Gamage. He was a delight, as he added his own stories and recollections using his unique animated style of Maine humor.

As we were wrapping things up for the second afternoon in a row, the cameras came out and the group hugs were overflowing. With the departure of our guests, the reunion at my parents' house came to a close. Seeing Dad sitting amongst the empty chairs in his living room, I questioned whether he felt a little let down after the excitement of the past two days. But no, he had a grin like one I had never seen on him before. I knew he had been given a gift that would last the rest of his days.

Whitehead Light Station, Maine, circa 1959
(Lane Family Collection)

Sandra, Russell, and Becky Lane at Whitehead Light Station in Maine
(Lane Family Collection)

Burleigh Hill Sailing Camp—Boothbay, Maine
(Anne Colclesser Faust Collection)

Burleigh Hill Sailing Camp-Group Picture 1958
(Anne Colclesser Faust Collection)

Susan Cheever, David Gamage, and Dan Granoff at my parents' house in Maine in May 2015 *(Lane Family Collection)*

Author and Peter Laylin with the Douglas C-124 Globemaster II at PIMA Air & Space Museum *(Lane Family Collection)*

Russell Lane, Russie Lane, and David Gamage at Whitehead Light Station
(Courtesy of Jeremy D'Entremont)

FRONT: Russell Lane   MIDDLE: Sandra Lane, Jeffrey Stark
BACK: Becky Lane Bryant, Heidi Ranger Lane, Russie Lane
(Courtesy of Chad Hanna)

CHAPTER 17

WHEN IT RAINS, IT POURS

They say that there are more BTUs in burning wood than in any other heat source. Of course, that is only if you cut it yourself. Each piece of wood warms you three or four times: once when you cut it, once when you split it, once when you stack it, and that is all before you even put it in the woodstove. I've heard tell of one frugal Mainer who kept warm all winter long with only one cord of wood; he didn't burn it, he just stacked it. That's how I was feeling about what little information I had on Leslie Lewis. It seemed I had gone over the pile so many times that I was just restacking it from one place to another.

There was something more that kept me in pursuit of Leslie. Something that called out to me beyond the Kodachrome and wouldn't let go. Leslie seemed to possess the innocence of a child and a sophistication beyond her seventeen years. She was someone who was so full of life and so close to death that I was intrigued by her experience and had to know her story.

But, for my own sanity, I also needed to try to accept the fact that Leslie might never be found. Life doesn't provide all the answers, wrapping everything up with a nice, pretty bow. The story and people I had uncovered so far resulted in a fun and welcome distraction from the disease that was demanding more of me as time marched along. I couldn't let the thought of never finding Leslie take away from the joy of finding the others and bringing them together.

The reunion with Susan and Dan seemed to breathe new life into everyone's efforts. Susan started digging more and came up with an old camper list with a note saying that Leslie's name was Leslie Ann Lewis. Even better than that, she found Leslie's home address, which was, indeed, in Lake Success. We even found her phone number, but it was strange-looking, an HU followed by four numbers. Even with my fear of telephones, you can bet that if I knew how to dial it, I would've made that call in a heartbeat.

Leslie's address was like a shot in the arm for the investigation. Oddly, it brought me to a story in the *Corpus Christi Caller-Times*:

UNWELCOME VISITOR—Boa Eludes Posse of Cautious Police

DATELINE: New York—Keeping a cautious distance away, a squad of special policemen hurled tear gas into a woodpile in Lake Success, L.I. yesterday. Then, guns at the ready and being careful where they stepped, they scattered the woodpile until there was no pile left. But their quarry had eluded them.

Once more, the big, tough-looking snake that has had the quiet Nassau County town in a dither for a week, had escaped... At least fifteen residents have reported him to the police... Kids have been kept off the streets... Those who have seen him say he is about ten feet long, about three to four inches in diameter. The description closely matches that of a ten-foot boa constrictor which escaped from a Bronx pet shop last August 14... The snake put in his latest appearance today in the backyard of John Lewis's home. Lewis's daughter, Leslie, fifteen, and a girlfriend, Irene Rook, twelve, were chipping a golf ball around the backyard to sharpen their game...

I couldn't believe my eyes! Did that really say *Lewis's daughter, Leslie?* After doing a double take, I continued reading.

One of them smacked the ball over the woodpile, and as they ran to retrieve it there was the snake, sticking his long neck and head out of the pile right next to the ball. The kids abandoned the ball and ran screaming into the house. Lewis, following the instructions issued to all residents when the snake first appeared, called the police. The police came with tear gas, but the snake had apparently slithered into the nearby woods.

The elusive Leslie Lewis had had an experience with an elusive snake. How fun was that?! Well, maybe not for them at the time, but it was an interesting discovery now. I hoped the *fun* would turn into something more functional now that I had a new person to search for

WHEN IT RAINS, IT POURS

in Leslie's neighbor, Irene Rook. With any luck, she might have kept in touch with Leslie. Inquiring minds needed to know.

I did find Irene's niece in short order. She informed me, sadly, that Irene had passed away. She also told me that her father remembered Leslie, but he hadn't had any contact with her in years. Alas, another trail had turned cold, but at least I had a chance to send her the snake story to share with her father. It would have been interesting to have heard the conversation around the Rook dinner table that evening. It must have given them second thoughts about going to the woodpile. (How long do snakes live, anyway?)

Days turned to weeks, and the end of May was fast approaching without any significant findings. Not that May was any deadline marked on a calendar. My calendar was clear except for a yearly eye appointment and semiannual dental cleaning. Yes, I do live an exceptionally exciting life.

The snake article in the Corpus Christi paper brought a chuckle and reminded me that you never know what you'll find on the Internet. Here it had been five months and I thought I had exhausted my resources. Just one new key word in a combination yielded an entirely new trail. With each step, new questions appeared waiting to be unlocked by the right combination of words typed into a search engine.

Leslie's father's first name and an old telephone book brought me to her mother's name. Her mother's name, along with the *New York Times*, brought me to the death notice of Leslie's mother and a very interesting thing: It mentioned the name of only one daughter, Terry. There was no mention of Leslie. Was Leslie a nickname? Maybe the wrong death notice? I retraced my steps, and all my bases were covered. It had to be her parents. Now I wasn't just stuck with the old question, Where's Leslie? I had a new one: Who is Terry?

Typing in the Lewises' old home address led to a boarding school in Connecticut that fortunately kept track of their alumni. Was I close to finding Leslie? I could feel it in my bones as I tracked Terry across the country and found her e-mail address. Like so many times before, all I could do was hit send and wait. I needed to share my discovery with Dan, Susan, and the rest of the kids, so I sent them an e-mail:

123

Pinch me! I am pretty certain I have found Leslie's sister. I am waiting for a reply.

Sending the e-mail wasn't enough to calm my desire to share the news. It was going on 11 p.m.—too late to call Susan, but Dan was on the West Coast, so I did the unthinkable (for me) and dialed Dan's number. When he answered, I found he wasn't in San Francisco but in Chicago. He was as excited as I was about the discovery. Now all we could do was to wait. The next day, I had a new arrival in my in-box. Excitedly, I opened the e-mail and felt jubilation as I read the first sentence:

I am the right person—that's the good news.

Uh-Oh, that's the good news. I prepared myself to swing a complete one hundred and eighty degrees with the next sentence:

The bad (news) is, my parents are long gone, my sister left home when I was eleven, and I've no idea where she is, what name she is using, anything.

As we corresponded over the next several days, Terry revealed a story that was terribly sad and in contrast to the lives of the other crew members aboard the sailboat *Debby*.

There has been so much heartbreak, so many lives made sadder by my sister's path in life. She abandoned everyone who cared about her, and those who needed her, too; disappeared and never looked back... My parents kept me in the dark about things until it was far too late to make a difference... I never knew the depths to which my sister sunk as a young adult until well after I had a family.

Terry wasn't sure whether Leslie ever went to college or even finished high school. Somewhere along the way, she ended up having two children out of wedlock with someone described as a "mafioso underling" who was already married and the father of five. When Leslie's parents tried to help her get out of the situation, their entire family was threatened, including Terry. Before she knew what had happened, Terry was taken out of the local school system and sent off to boarding school in Connecticut. Her summers were spent at various camps. (In hindsight, this was her parents' attempt to keep her safe and out of harm's way.) Terry was not really sure when it happened, but Leslie stopped in at her parents' home one day and left a note that read, "I'm trapped. I'm leaving. Goodbye."

Her father made it clear to Terry that "there was real danger in trying to find Leslie." At that point, Terry thinks her parents simply gave up. Years passed without hearing from or seeing her sister. Then, somewhere around 1975, Leslie appeared unannounced at Terry's house. Her name had changed, and she was living somewhere in Texas. She stayed for about a half hour, then got up and walked out the door. Terry has not seen her since.

Summing up her story, she wrote:

I am a happy mother and grandmother, and about to celebrate my 35th anniversary with my husband. My family means more to me than anything.

As for strength, my dear friend who is getting over some heavy-duty cancer treatment just said last week, "We do what we have to [in order] to survive"; I consider myself very lucky to be living the life I am.

Ironically, Terry said she thanks her sister because it seemed to wake her parents up and got Terry away from an unhealthy family life.

Those few days corresponding with Leslie's sister had revealed a heartbreaking story, taking a path I had not expected. I felt endeared to Terry and admired her perseverance. However, I felt sad to have dredged up old memories for her, ones she had already dealt with. I hoped she would forgive me for the intrusion. There was a lot for me to process over the next few days.

As the week progressed, we received word from Senator Collins's office about the findings of the Coast Guard investigation. They had discovered that my father had indeed been recommended years ago for a commendation. That was the good news. But unfortunately, he did not qualify for any commendation back then or now. Though

SNOW ANGELS ON THE MOON

disappointed by the news, my parents' reaction did not surprise me. They were more upset about the news concerning Leslie.

It wasn't all bad news from Senator Collins's office, though. In recognition of his service and actions on the day of the rescue, Senator Collins wanted to send Dad a letter and a flag that had flown over the Capitol building. Dad liked that idea and felt honored. Clearly, the quest for recognition for my father had come to an end. The kids who were rescued were unhappy with the decision of the Coast Guard, but they accepted it. Looking back, it had stopped being about finding recognition for Dad a long time ago.

CHAPTER 18

A TALE OF TWO ISLANDS

Isn't it funny how two completely different places can conjure up the same feelings? The next couple of weeks could be described as "a tale of two islands." Separated by only a few hundred miles, I found these two small land masses surrounded by water to be worlds apart. One, inhabited by a sea of people, is the most expensive real estate on the planet, Manhattan, while the other lies dormant most of the year off the Maine coast, only to be visited by a trickle of souls each summer. In the name of preservation, its visitors are like members of a secret society who would never divulge the existence of this gem that is Whitehead Island. About to experience both places, I couldn't decide if I was more excited or scared. One thing I did know, though: Each would take me in a different direction. Yet somehow I would end up at the same destination—somewhere outside of my comfort zone.

It was the Wednesday morning before the July 4th holiday weekend. Heidi and I had just passed through security at Portland Jetport on our way to New York City. I was still feeling guilty about not taking her on my trip to the West Coast. It felt good to make up for it at least a little by treating her to a few days in Manhattan and a Broadway show. Sprinkle in a couple of meetings with some Burleigh Hill campers, and this promised to be an exciting time.

Waiting for the announcement to board the plane, Heidi raced to finish her morning coffee while I brought out my phone and started checking messages. It had become a habit born more out of boredom than anything. Mindlessly swiping, I alternated between opening and deleting each message.

Wait a minute, what did I just delete? Did that say Whitehead Light Station? I dived headfirst into the trash folder and rummaged for

SNOW ANGELS ON THE MOON

what I had just thrown away. Yup, sure enough, there it was—a reply from Whitehead. I had contacted them earlier in the week telling them about my father's story and my endeavor to document it. It just so happened that they had a retreat scheduled the following weekend and they had one room available. I was welcome to come, explore the island, and take as much video as I wanted. Up until now, I had only used still photos, but this opportunity would enable me to take my slide show to the next level and make it into a movie! It doesn't hurt to dream, does it?

Heidi informed me she had to work those days, but she encouraged me to take them up on the offer and to go along without her. I replied right then and there. I was all booked for Whitehead before Heidi had time to finish her coffee. Just as slick as a smelt. Don't you love technology?!

Our plane arrived at JFK airport on time, and little did we know we were about to undertake the most dangerous part of our trip. The half-hour van ride that transported us from the airport to the hotel was the longest, most terrifying ride of my life. We passengers were packed in like a can of Port Clyde sardines and the van's air conditioner blew only hot, stifling air. The driver (let's call him Evel Knievel) was so erratic behind the wheel he had us literally bouncing off one another. Weaving through and around traffic, I saw my life flash before my eyes again and again.

We arrived at the Sofitel New York on West 44th Street, and I could finally catch my breath. Dripping with perspiration from head to toe, it was all I could do to pry my fingertips from the back of the seat. The driver was out in a flash, throwing our bags in a heap and then standing quietly with palm extended. Handing him a sweaty, crumpled dollar bill, I was probably too generous, but I was just thankful to have survived the ordeal.

The sidewalk was the prettiest sight of the whole trip to that point. Better than that, it was solid under my feet and felt safe—well, solid, anyway. I never truly feel safe anywhere south of Kittery, but that is the Mainer in me, the one who moves his wallet to his front pocket the minute he crosses the Maine/New Hampshire border.

A TALE OF TWO ISLANDS

After checking in at the hotel, we dropped off our bags at the room and decided to explore the city. As we made our way up the sidewalk, it became apparent we weren't the only people who had decided to visit New York this day. With one hand on my wallet and one eye on Heidi, we squeezed through the meat grinder that is Times Square. I had never been so intimate with so many people at once in my life. All I could think about was buying hand sanitizer and dousing myself with it. Through it all, Heidi was beaming from the experience. I was glad at least one of us was having fun.

I am not sure where we popped out of the migrating mass of people, but we somehow navigated a big loop ending back at the hotel. I needed a shower and a little downtime before meeting Tim Jerome for dinner.

Gazing out the 20th-something-floor window of our room, I felt a little trapped. Was it claustrophobia or a twinge of 9/11? I wasn't sure. No matter what, I had to get over it. Putting that out of my mind, I got lost in the awesome view. I had never felt so insignificant yet so in awe of the grandeur of a skyline. Amongst the shiny and new, the tops of older buildings sported wooden water towers that could have come straight out of an old western movie. The contrast spoke volumes. Even in this modern world, some of the old tried-and-true ways are still the best options.

Moving from the window, I did my best to ignore the claustrophobia that tried to claw its way back to my consciousness. How do people live like this? It was at that point Heidi noticed a picture on the wall. It was of a lighthouse with five seagulls on the roof—one for each kid rescued. Could this be a coincidence, or was it a sign that we were where we should be? My vote must have sided with the latter, as I calmed down enough to fall asleep. Heidi woke me from my nap just in time to leave for dinner. The claustrophobic feeling vanished, never to return for the rest of the trip.

On the way down in the elevator, I clicked the restaurant's address Tim had provided in his e-mail, and up popped directions. Heidi and I hit the streets of the Big Apple. I walked as if I knew where I was going. Everybody did. I wondered if they were blindly being led by their cell phones, as well. The only downfall to this plan was that if my phone

129

were to die, we'd be lost in transit. Worse than that, panic set in as I realized if it *did* die, I couldn't even tell you the name of the restaurant. However, the phone did its job, and we arrived a good fifteen minutes early.

Just like before my first meeting with Dan, standing still was not an option. I started pacing. Now, if someone would just hand me a picket sign or a sandwich board, I could make better use of my steps. But until that happened, I was content walking guard duty and scanning the crowd for Tim Jerome.

Tim had not been on the ill-fated *Debby* the afternoon of the rescue, but he was one of the campers that made it to Tenants Harbor. I was excited to meet him and discuss his Burleigh Hill memories. Heidi was just as excited, but hers stemmed more from going to see Tim perform as Monsieur Firmin in *The Phantom of the Opera.*

When he stepped out of the crowd, Tim and I made eye contact at the same time. He challenged me with a word that no one else on that sidewalk could possibly know. "Russ?"

I responded right back with the counterchallenge, "Tim?"

I would have known him anywhere. He still carried around that infectious smile from his childhood. I introduced him to Heidi. After greeting her warmly, he led us into the restaurant. He apologized to the host who met us at the door, saying he did not have reservations but was hoping for a table. Then it came, just like a line from a movie. "That's okay, Mr. Jerome. We always have a table for you."

The three of us were seated and immediately engaged in conversation. The topics bounced from Burleigh Hill to lighthouses to presidential politics. I had been hoping more memories might have been shaken loose in Tim's head since I had contacted him last. However, the discussion about camp days didn't last long. Dinner went by too fast. As we were about to leave, I presented Tim with a Burleigh Hill Camp hat. He put it on immediately and his youthful smile grew all the wider. Soon we were outside the restaurant taking group selfies.

The street was more than busy; it was mobbed. Tim led the way to the theater and explained how to meet up with him after the show. He disappeared through the stage door. Heidi and I enjoyed the sights and sounds of Broadway as nighttime came to the city without darkness. Strangely, things only got brighter as the time neared to enter the theater. *The Phantom of the Opera* did not disappoint, and we saw firsthand why it is the longest-running Broadway show. Making our way against the crowd as the show ended, we waited at the foot of the stage according to Tim's instructions. We blinked, and the backstage tour was done. As Tim walked us back in the direction of our hotel, he explained that we would part ways with two blocks to go. However, he asked that we e-mail him after we were safely back in the hotel. His concern for our well-being was genuine, and as he disappeared into the crowd I truly hoped that would not be the last we would see of Mr. Tim Jerome.

Reminiscent of my San Francisco marathon, Heidi and I were up early the next morning to start exploring. My well-worn sneakers, the same pair that had served me so nobly then, were ready to tackle New York City. I wish I could have said the same thing about Heidi's choice of footwear. Her sandals were more for fashion than function.

As we rounded every corner, we encountered something else familiar. We had no idea we knew so much about New York City. I suppose that's a testimony to the power and influence of TV and film. I wouldn't have believed it if you'd told me that one of the highlights of the morning would have been sitting on a bench in Central Park. It wasn't just the green space, it was such a delight to sit and watch young people enjoying the time. That's something we lack in Maine: young people. Some think our biggest export is lobster, but in actuality it is our youth. We do a good job at raising and educating them, but we fall short at providing them opportunities or reasons to stay around afterwards. "Fifty Shades of Grey" isn't just a steamy book. When it comes to Maine, it best describes the majority of hair color at our local town meetings.

By the time we arrived to meet Susan at the Metropolitan Museum of Art, Heidi's sandals were taking a toll. She wasn't complaining but took advantage of the time to rest her feet and soothe her blisters while we waited on the steps.

It took us a few moments to notice, but Susan was already on the steps behind us when we sat down. She hadn't seen us, and we

SNOW ANGELS ON THE MOON

didn't see her. It gave us something to laugh about as we went into the museum. Being the quintessential New Yorker, Susan kept us thoroughly entertained as she showed us around the museum. The Cheever Charm was in full swing as we enjoyed a sit-down lunch in the atrium and discussed new discoveries about Burleigh Hill. Susan had found some childhood letters stashed away in her mother's attic. One was even from Lester Rhoads on camp letterhead explaining what had taken place on Mussel Ridge. Apparently, the campers had caused $500 worth of damage to the sailboat during the "incident."

After finishing the meal, Susan asked what we wanted to see in the museum. I asked her to show us the exhibits that meant the most to her. We saw the world on display that afternoon, and now I understand why the Metropolitan Museum of Art draws so many visitors.

Seeing the painting of *Washington Crossing the Delaware* blew me away. It had to measure twenty feet wide or more. We were dwarfed by its immensity. It made me wonder how an artist can keep perspective on the big picture, all while being within an arm's reach of the canvas.

As the afternoon came to a close, I was glad that Susan would join us for dinner at the Century Association, where we would meet with Jeff Stark. I deferred to Susan to see if I needed to wear a jacket and tie. She added to my concern with the last part of her response, "Yes, a jacket and tie and a VERY serious expression on your face!" Probably seeing my shock, she smiled, explaining that she was just kidding, there were no worries. The Century Association had been her father's club, and she said, "I have misbehaved there enough for all of us over the years." She assured me it was a nice, quiet place to have dinner and talk about Burleigh Hill.

We parted ways on the museum's steps, and as Susan hailed a cab, Heidi and I found 5th Avenue and started our trek back to the hotel. I have no idea why we didn't follow Susan's lead and catch a cab ourselves. Heidi's feet would have been grateful for the consideration.

Finally getting back to the hotel, my body felt tired. Fortunately, we didn't have far to walk for dinner. Two months earlier, I had made reservations at the hotel way before any mention of meeting Jeff Stark or dinner at the Century Club. Punching the address into my phone, I was surprised to find out that it was right across the street and around the block, a three, maybe four-minute walk at the most. As with so many happenings over the last six months, things just fell into place.

Dinner at the prestigious Century Association in New York City sounded intriguing on the surface, but it was all I could do to bolster the courage to walk through the doors. Of course, it helped having Heidi along for the trip. I feared anyone I encountered would hear the echo of my heart beating wildly in the ever-expanding hall. The rich wood grains and priceless artwork lining the walls spoke of an affluence and history that intimidated me to no end. On the far side of the room, two small figures descended the grand staircase and walked in our direction. We walked toward them to meet in the middle of the hall. The closer they came, the more I could make out that the figures approaching were Susan and, I assumed, Jeff. My eyes fixated on their smiles. The corners of my mouth gave a mirrored response, and all tension dissipated from my body. The cold, staunch walls ceased their running from me, and the room began to shrink to a calming size. Maybe this place wasn't as far out of my comfort zone as I'd feared. Oh, the power of a smile!

Jeff had a firm, welcoming grip when he reached out to shake my hand, while Susan warmly hugged Heidi. I was carrying a gift bag to give to Jeff. He assumed it was mine and led me to the coatroom, offering me a cubby for safekeeping. It reminded me of my cubby from third grade, which seemed comforting at that moment. I explained it was a present for him, so he accepted the bag and we returned to where Susan and Heidi had been waiting for us.

Touring around the building, I couldn't decide if it was more library or art museum. The beautiful tall wooden bookshelves were equipped with ladders on rollers, but I was thinking they were used more for dusting than getting a book down to read. Jeff explained that in lieu of yearly membership fees, artists such as Winslow Homer would offer a painting to add to their walls. In its earlier days, it was named the Century Association because its rolls were limited to one hundred members.

As we took our seats in the dining room, we were the only four guests in the building as far as I could tell. At one point, the staff

SNOW ANGELS ON THE MOON

outnumbered us around the table. After making several suggestions, Jeff ordered dinner for the group and the staff disappeared into the woodwork.

Susan, forever the cheerleader and having heard many of my stories before, coached me on which ones to share. We were laughing around the table and everyone was at ease. At least, I know I was. Soon Jeff joined in with his own stories. While the other "kids" had buried the traumatic experience and seldom talked about the rescue over the years, Jeff told the story hundreds of times to anyone who would listen. He said he had never been so cold in his life, but didn't think he was going to die that day.

The conversation about the rescue continued, and I discovered that Jeff was the one responsible for remembering many of the details. Much like the game of telephone, where you whisper a message in the next kid's ear, the memories trickled down to me. Dan had earlier credited Susan. However, that evening, Susan said that many of the detailed memories she had passed along had come from Jeff.

Somewhere along the way, the topic turned to Maine and hiking. It turned out Jeff liked climbing even more than I did. He had hiked many of the trails at Acadia National Park including the Precipice, which is a bit too scary for me, since others have died attempting it. To my surprise, Jeff confided that he had a fear of heights. There was a lesson somewhere in there to ponder; something about not letting your fears stop you from facing life's challenges.

As the evening ended, the four of us made our way out onto the street. Susan went off in one direction and Jeff took Heidi and me along in the other. The gentleman in me wanted to see that Susan made it into a cab safely, but this was her turf and she assured me she would be okay. We continued our visit with Jeff as we walked along. He hoped to someday plan a visit to my parents, but for the time being asked that we give them his best. As we reached the end of the block, he shook my hand and disappeared down the busy sidewalk.

Arriving back at the hotel, I hated to go to bed knowing we would have to leave in the morning. We had packed a lot into our last day in Manhattan. When I checked my messages one last time, I saw there was one from Susan asking if we had made it back safely to our hotel and thanking us for our visit. I couldn't help but concur with her assessment as I read the last line of her message: *"This really has been quite a New York day."*

CHAPTER 19

BACK WHERE I BEGAN

Going to summer camp was not on my radar growing up. I did go to camp one year, though, but I wasn't very happy about it. It was a church camp in the middle of the state on some lake up past Augusta. My mother somehow convinced Dad that he could live without me for a week on the lobster boat. I was secretly rooting for him to say no—after all, it was at the height of fishing—but he buckled under the pressure and I was headed off to camp.

Being dropped off at camp promised to be an awful experience, at least as it was playing out in my mind beforehand. Not that I would feel abandoned or homesick, but I knew I would need to open my mouth to introduce myself. I often wonder what happened that first day of camp. It must have not been that bad because the only thing I remember now was the torture I put myself through before arriving there. The whole week must have been pretty uneventful, except there was that one night sleeping under the stars.

We were a small group of boys and girls, all about the same age, from opposing tents. Someone in the group—probably some young, budding astronomer-type—had the bright idea to sleep outside under the stars. One of the girls, the prettiest one in the bunch, I might add, was the only one smart enough to bring a pillow. The counselor allowed her to share that one pillow with the group as long as the boys stayed on one side and girls stayed on the other. We lay in a circle, with all heads pointing toward the center and converging on a little piece of pillow.

Sleeping on the ground was not my idea of what summer camp should be. But, upon looking up at the sky, I was quickly sold on the idea. If God had a Rembrandt moment, this was it. His canvas was

SNOW ANGELS ON THE MOON

painted with the blackest black. There was a thin sliver of moon carved in the right-hand, upper corner. It must have been accomplished using a fine brush. The moon had just enough of a hook on the bottom with which to hang your hat or your hopes, whichever you carried. If the Artist were to stop there, it would still be a testimony that even in a world of darkness the tiniest of light demands one's eye. But instead of leaving it at that simple message, with a quick flick of the brush, a gazillion stars were splattered in the sky, each precisely placed to pin a wish on.

When I was a kid in the 1960s, there were two stories that were making the news every night: one that seemed to be tearing the world apart, Vietnam, and the other that was bringing the world together, our endeavor to walk on the moon. So it was kind of fitting that looking up at the evening sky is what brought these young campers together in the field that night. Of course, the astronauts couldn't have landed on the moon on a night such as this. Since the moon was reduced to a sliver, they would need to wait until it was full to provide a bigger target to land on.

As I lay looking up at the heavens, I was mesmerized. Maybe that's why I didn't sleep much that night...although it could have been attributed to the hardness of the ground or the coolness of the evening, I wasn't really sure. Then again, maybe my imagination concocted the thought of hungry bears rummaging through the trash cans at the dining hall. Would we offer them a detour and become their dessert as we lay in this field in the middle of the night?

There was so much to blame my sleeplessness on, and it was difficult to pin it down to one thing. The experience would have been unbearable except for one small source of comfort—the piece of pillow I had claimed. Sometime in the night—I was trying to get to sleep by counting the twinkles in my favorite star—to my surprise, my nearest neighbor, Pillow Girl, crossed the pillow property line and rested her head against mine. Grateful for what territory she shared, and being the gentleman that I was, I surrendered more space. It wasn't long before she claimed even more of the area I had vacated. Was her head walking in its sleep? Was she scared of those pesky bears? No worries here; I would protect her. I wasn't sure if it was lack of chivalry or my advancing puberty to blame, but I lay motionless the rest of the evening, refusing to give up any more space. I passed time exploring the sky, listening for hungry bears, and letting her head rest against mine. As dawn approached, Pillow Girl awoke and moved her head away. It was the saddest sunrise I ever saw.

———————

Fast forward forty-plus years: I sat in my truck alone at the water's edge and had that scary sensation of being dropped off at summer camp again. Looking out at Whitehead Island looming on the horizon a mile or so off the mainland, I wondered if this Rest & Relaxation Getaway weekend was such a good idea after all. It was a great opportunity to experience the island that my mother and father had called home for two years. My only connection with Whitehead was through Dad's stories and his reassuring claim that I was conceived there. Probably for some people that was too much information. After all, there is no space on a job application to write one's place of conception, but I was kind of proud of it.

As an added bonus, I would be spending three days with people whom I did not know, and more importantly for a stutterer, people who did not know me. There would be questions, and I would need to provide answers, *out loud*. The thought made my hands cold and clammy even though the thermometer in the truck was climbing past eighty degrees. My heart started to race on a track it knew well. Trying to keep myself calm, I didn't notice the older couple getting out of the car behind me until I heard their car door close. The gentleman approached me first, with a smile wider than my anxiety.

"Hi... Are you going out to Whitehead lighthouse?" he asked. He looked harmless enough.

"Yup," I nodded. That was easy, I thought to myself. The ice was broken. I then turned to the lady following close behind him.

"Good morning."

"Good morning!" she greeted back. "What a beautiful day." Her smile was bigger than her companion's. It did not stop at her mouth but radiated from her entire being. She introduced herself as Olga, a fitting

SNOW ANGELS ON THE MOON

name for such a petite, capri-clad lady. I could not decide if she was elf-like or more of a fairy princess. I was certain of one thing, though: Olga could light up any space she occupied.

As we continued to chat, I learned that the man's name was Jerry and they were newlyweds. Once high school sweethearts, they had found each other again later in life after losing their spouses. You could tell they adored one another. Jerry would talk about Olga and Olga talked about Jerry, calling each other by name. It was perfect for someone like me who always had trouble remembering people's names. By the end of the conversation, I knew Jerry and Olga quite well.

Another lady joined the group, and we exchanged names and life stories in the first ten minutes. Of course, I had to include my quest to uncover facts about the rescue and my father in the conversation. I wondered if they noticed my speech problem—not my stuttering, but my other one that can be more annoying. Once you get me talking, it can be a hard job to shut me up.

Now what was *that* lady's name again? What does it matter anyway? Meeting these people wasn't why I was coming to this island.

The boat arrived at the dock and the young gentleman at the helm stepped off the boat and introduced himself. I jumped on his name. *Matt, Matt, Matt.* How can I remember his name is Matt?

As we carried our luggage to the boat, I was still trying to commit the captain's name to memory. Matt Dillon? No. Matt Damon? No. Let's see, he was the first person to greet us with a welcoming smile, to roll out the red carpet, the welcome mat. *Welcome Matt*; got it, that'll work. I was glad no one could hear the word association going on in my head. Okay, we have Olga, Jerry, Matt, and What's-her-name. Well, three out of four isn't bad. Soon we had loaded all the gear aboard and Captain "Welcome" Matt cast off the lines. For the next twenty minutes, the roar of the outboard motor curtailed any further speech, for which I was always grateful, no matter what the gathering. I wasn't being anti-social; I just knew I had a job to do. I didn't want to be distracted by small talk as we traveled the mile from the mainland out to the island. I wanted to clear my mind and press "record" on my senses and then see what stuck.

140

As we snaked around the moorings and dodged the lobstermen tending their traps, I was seeing things with fresh eyes. I had grown up around the water in a harbor much like this one. That boat ride should have been nothing special, but it was. I hadn't realized how much I missed being out on the water.

Enough of this living for the moment; I couldn't allow myself to be distracted from my work. Going over the checklist in my mind, I was hoping I hadn't forgotten any of my equipment. Oh, well, if I did, there was nothing I could do about it now. I just needed to trust that I had prepared myself enough for the trip. After all, I had done my research. I could spout off the particulars without hesitation like reading the stats off a baseball card.

Player's Name: Whitehead Light Station. **Rookie Year:** *commissioned by Thomas Jefferson 1803, built 1807.* **Tower Height:** *41 feet.* **Beacon:** *Occulting—green with a flash of darkness every 4 seconds.* **Fog signal:** *2 blasts every 30 seconds.* **Bats** *right,* **Throws** *left.*

Fun Facts: Whitehead Light Station lies along the Maine coast, halfway between Portland and Mount Desert Island. For over two centuries, it has welcomed ships to Penobscot Bay, but, more importantly, safely guided them up Mussel Ridge Channel, a route between the mainland and a chain of islands that offer sheltered passage away from the open ocean.

Now, as we approached Whitehead Island, I was not prepared for the surge of emotions that rose up like the running tide. Matt brought back the throttle to an idle. As the shoreline came into focus, my father's stories came to life. I could see it all from the water: the granite dock where the lobster boat *Mabel*, lady-in-waiting to be used for the rescue, had once been tied. And there was the boathouse with the ramp my father built and the path that disappeared into the woods that led to the lighthouse on the other side of the island. I reached down deep to fight back the tears, but it was futile. A hand came from nowhere and rested on my shoulder. I looked up and saw caring eyes and a tight-lipped smile from a newfound friend, the lady with no name. Were my emotions that obvious, or was she so perceptive that

SNOW ANGELS ON THE MOON

she sensed my feelings? Either way, I was grateful for this person with a gentle touch.

As the captain flipped the bumpers over the railing to cushion our landing, he eased up to the float, grabbed the lines, and tied up. It was time to gather my composure, step off the boat, and go back to where I began.

CHAPTER 20

EVERYBODY NEEDS A NAME

Reaching down to pick up a few pieces of my equipment, a voice from behind asked me to please leave everything where it was and go up on the dock. I turned around to see it was Matt. His request to leave the bags alone wasn't from the voice of authority. Rather, it was centered in hospitality.

"This is no weekend for heavy lifting," he explained.

My eyes protested while my lips lay silent. "Oh, I'm not one of *them*. This is a working weekend for me."

His kind eyes answered back, reflecting in the true fashion of his position. There would be no debate. These were captain's orders; it was time to relax and enjoy the weekend.

It was almost impossible to comply with Matt's wishes as I scaled the ramp and waited on the dock. I just hadn't been brought up that way. "Many hands make light work" kept playing over in my mind as I watched Matt carry my equipment over several trips. I easily had three times more luggage than anyone else. People must have thought I was staying for two weeks when in actuality it mostly contained my technology. It consisted of my iPhone, iPad, laptop, eight different cameras and lenses, tripods, and a microphone, not to mention clothes and essentials for the weekend. Who was I kidding? They *all* were my essentials. However, I did worry if some might consider my equipment to be contraband. After all, everyone had spent big money to leave society, technology, and their troubles behind for the weekend, and here I was bringing every ounce of technology with me. Well, not every ounce; I did opt out on the flying drone with the attached camera. It really didn't have a purpose for this trip.

The words *purpose for this trip* stopped me in my thoughts. All of a sudden, my guilt melted away, leaving only gratefulness. Matt knew what he was doing in refusing my help. He was freeing me, or should I say, all of us, to do what we came for, whether that be rest, relaxation, or getting to work.

Breaking off from the group, I stood there taking in the island one sense at a time. Like a detective in a crime scene, I analyzed everything. Closing my eyes, my other senses stepped to the plate to take up the slack. The light wind brushing past the trees behind me, like vocal cords, gave a continuous whisper-like sound to the island. The waves rhythmically lapped a soft drumbeat on the shore. The cackling gulls playfully soaring overhead provided the lyrics. With my ears full and my eyes remaining closed, I inhaled deeply. The smell of the evergreens mixed with salt air took hold of my nostrils. But wait. There was something else. I exhaled, completely clearing my lungs of any excess toxins that I might have inadvertently brought with me. I inhaled again; there it was. Just a slight hint of low tide. It wasn't a bad smell, just a natural, manly sort of combination. *Ruddy*, an island fragrance for men. There, I thought to myself, I have the formula set. Now all I have to do is figure out how to bottle it and we'll be ready to market.

Laughter from across the dock broke over me in mid-thought. The group seemed to be having a fun time. What was I missing? There would be enough time over the next three days to explore and analyze the island. I walked over to join the group, bound and determined not to miss another chance to be in on the laughter.

As the last of our baggage was loaded into the John Deere Gator, there was only room for one passenger. We all agreed with our feet as we walked away that Olga—my fairy princess friend—would get the ride. The remaining three of us started up the road that led into the woods. With each step, I took in more of the island, every rock, every tree, every sound. There was one special thing I was hoping to key in on, and my senses were on high alert until I discovered it.

Then it happened. The sound of the four-wheeler from behind brought a warning from Jerry. "Watch out, Pat!"

I snatched the name out of the air and tossed it back and forth in my mind like I was juggling a hot potato. Pat, Pat...Pat, Pat.

EVERYBODY NEEDS A NAME

We split apart and waited on the sides of the road as Captain Matt and Olga passed on by. My mind went to work...a comforting smile and a pat on my shoulder when I needed it most... That's it! That's easy enough to remember. We joined back in the middle of the road.

"That was a close one, wasn't it, Pat?" I said, testing out her name.

"It certainly was, Russ."

And there it was. Confirmation from the lady with no name, the person who will now forever be known as Pat. I felt better; everybody on the island had a name.

As we broke out of the woods, my eyes became fixated on the vast wide-open Atlantic and the lighthouse that stood watch over it. Stopping for a moment to take it all in, I wished I could have brought my parents along with me. But the reality of it told me no. Dad was just too frail and unsteady on his feet to get aboard the boat, let alone get around while on the island. Not wanting to miss anything fun, I ran to catch up with my new buddies, Pat and Jerry.

Gigi, the island manager, greeted us at the door with the offer of iced tea and cookies in the dining room. She then directed us upstairs to our rooms, where Matt had already delivered our bags. The view outside my window showed a different "high-rise" than the ones in last week's view of Manhattan. Both, however, were equally breathtaking in their own ways. This week's scene was straight from the heart of Andrew Wyeth. The shaded white metal foot-post of my bed showed in sharp contrast as the sunlight flowed through an open curtain. The tall granite tower stood only a few feet outside the window, holding a green beacon on high to greet boats by day. It transforms into a flickering flame by night that has guided ships and sailors safely for centuries. Twenty yards away from the tower, the rocks disappear into the ocean. Twenty yards more, and a sailboat was lazily just coming into view. This was Maine at its best.

My room was exquisitely simple, with a handwritten welcome card on the bed along with a towel folded up into a swan. It made me wish I'd brought my own towel so I could have left him undisturbed next to me for the weekend. Venturing down the stairs, I explored the rest of the house. The rooms were bright and cheery with wingback chairs and comfortable couches. A library full of Maine books and lightkeeper journals was there for rainy days or lazy afternoons. Settling down in a chair with an iced tea and a cookie, I knew I was going to like it here.

Once outside, I was free to roam over every inch of the lighthouse and the surrounding area. I was like a kid on a playground. Climbing to the top of the tower, I could get a good perspective on what had happened the day of the rescue. From this vantage point, I could picture my mother down along the shore picking berries and my father hidden in the hollow off to my right pitching horseshoes. Halfway up toward the horizon, a sinking sailboat wouldn't look much bigger than a speck out there. Add a feather-white chop to the tops of the waves, and the people in the water would have easily blended in, going unnoticed. The odds of being rescued would have been heavily against them. The word *miracle* was the only one that came to mind. Some might say the campers were lucky to survive that day, damn lucky. Dad had always made his feelings known about their chances, saying, "If we'd counted on luck that day, no one would have survived."

Turning my attention to the lighthouse, it looked good for its age. But it hadn't always been that way. Automation had taken away the need for lightkeepers and their quarters. Soon the head keeper's house on the hill was dismantled and the main house, a duplex next to the tower, was boarded up and abandoned. Unfortunately, demolition was the fate of many orphaned lighthouses strewn along the coast and forgotten by the population. Just across Mussel Ridge Channel was a prime example, Two Bush Island Light. The lone tower now stands on a barren island that no longer has the signature two clumps of trees that birthed its name, and its keeper's house is long gone, used for explosive demolition practice by the U.S. Army Green Berets in 1970.

What was left of Whitehead Light Station could have suffered the same fate if not for the help of a generous benefactor, the Pine Island Boys Camp out of Belgrade Lakes. Owned and operated by the Swan family for over a hundred years, the camp petitioned the Coast Guard for the property and now owns and maintains Whitehead Light Station.

EVERYBODY NEEDS A NAME

It seems ironic that the lighthouse responsible for saving the lives of five from a summer camp in 1958 was, itself, later saved by another Maine camp.

As the afternoon progressed, two more guests arrived, two more names to remember. A little later, the clanging bell outside on the porch caught the ear of everyone on this end of the island. Bookmarks were slid between pages, Adirondack chairs vacated, and those on a leisurely hike in the nearby woods abandoned the trail. We all converged on the keeper's house to experience a gourmet creation disguised under the simple name of "dinner" that Gigi had prepared. Being our hostess, our chef, the island manager, our tour director, and our all-around "house-mother" for the weekend, Gigi wore many hats.

Sitting around a large table, we ate family-style. Mealtimes became the highlight. It turned out that Olga was quite a storyteller, and we began a friendly competition trying to outdo one another across the table.

I'm not sure when the magic began, but I assume it was in stepping off the boat. The weekend became less about my mission to capture the essence of the island on film, and more about experiencing White-head and enjoying everyone's company. But I still accomplished what I came for. I don't think I missed an angle or time of day during my filming. I was up in the wee hours shooting video and went to bed at midnight after reviewing it. The weather was picture-perfect. Every-thing was beautiful. Every breath was sweet. Every morsel of food brought moans of delight around the dinner table. We reached a comfort level that felt like family.

On our final afternoon on the island, I found myself sitting down on the rocks with Olga. We were still trying to outdo each other's stories. The conversation took a serious tone. She told me she had spent a life-time listening to more than her share of stories. As a stenographer for the White House, she had hand-delivered her transcripts to the Oval Office every day as part of the Watergate hearings. Through it all, there was one thing she had learned: everyone has a story to tell. She then looked me in the eye and said, "But yours is different, it needs to be heard."

As the time came to leave the island that afternoon, I knew it was going to be tough. The weekend had been like going to summer camp.

SNOW ANGELS ON THE MOON

If I had become this close to my new friends after three days, what would it have been like for the Burleigh Hill campers who ate, slept, and breathed camp with each other for eight weeks?

We gave our goodbye hugs to Jerry and Olga before leaving the lighthouse. They were scheduled to spend a few more days. Gigi walked us down to the dock, where she stood waving as we pushed away in the boat.

With the weekend all but over, it was time to go back to reality. Or was it? Seeing a piece of rope thrown over in the corner, I sized up the situation: four against one. We could overpower Matt, tie him up, and turn the vessel about. I wasn't sure what the penalty might be for mutiny on the high seas in 2015. What's the worst they could do, make us walk the plank? It seemed a small price to pay for one more day of magic on Whitehead Island.

CHAPTER 21

ON HOLD

As July was drawing to a close, the world was put on hold—or at least my little part of it. There were no thoughts of the rescue or Burleigh Hill or Whitehead Light Station. My daughter, Amanda, was about to undertake a role she had been preparing for her whole life: motherhood. She had barely learned to talk when she was watching herd over "the babies," as she called them. They were her twin cousins Aimee and April, who were actually one week her senior. She never missed an opportunity to mother the people around her, even at that young age.

Sadly, the previous September, Amanda and her husband, Jon, had suffered the loss of their first baby during premature labor. According to the doctors, there were complicated issues that couldn't be detected until it was too late. Little Emilia was the trailblazer whose sacrifice paved the way for her baby brother. Still a high-risk pregnancy, all Heidi and I could do was wait and pray, a primary role of prospective grandparents since the beginning of time.

When word came that Dietrich Oliver Morningstar had arrived, Heidi and I loaded into the car and were on our way to Pennsylvania. We tried making good use of the twelve-hour drive. It gave us time to reminisce about our own children and prepare ourselves to be grandparents.

I recalled proudly holding my daughter for the first time and feared she would break like a porcelain doll. And then there was my son, Drew, two years later. He was all boy. Born on the Fourth of July. Mr. Independent from day one. I think if we had given him the choice to stand up and walk out of the delivery room, he would've done so.

The longest part of the trip was walking from the car into the hospital to find Amanda's room. After navigating the maze of corridors, we arrived. Standing in the hallway, I peered silently through the door. I was witness to a pure Norman Rockwell moment: a young mother holding her baby tenderly in her arms while a proud father stood by the bed. Heidi, though, had waited long enough. She shattered the scene and barged into the room. She just *had* to hold that baby!

While patiently waiting for my turn to hold Dietrich, I realized I had forgotten how small babies can be. At quarter past the hour, Amanda scooped him away from Heidi like a referee at a football game and gave him to me. In my arms, he became even smaller. At this stage, as a newborn, he was pretty helpless—at least that's what I thought until he reached out and grabbed my thumb. He held on for dear life, and I could tell this kid had some strength.

There was a lesson to be learned in that little hand gripping my thumb. We all face times when our only option is to hold on for dear life. Whether it's holding onto a sinking sailboat or holding onto the hope of finding a cure for a medical condition like Parkinson's. I had so much to teach this young grandson of mine, but maybe I had just better keep still and see what I could learn from him first.

It was a fun first week of grandparenthood, but the time came when we had to think about heading back to Maine. Looking at the map, I noticed we were "only" five hours from Rochester, where camp counselor and boat captain Annie lived. I proposed to Heidi that we leave a day early and take a detour to visit Annie. Soon we were crossing the border on our way to Upstate New York.

The closer we came to Rochester, the more our excitement grew— along with nervousness, I might add. Annie's house was located on the banks of a tributary leading to Lake Ontario. As we drove into her driveway, both the entrance and the house had the feel of something out of *Swiss Family Robinson*. The building could best be described as a tree house constructed on many levels, covered in ivy and surrounded by trees. It was difficult to tell where the branches began and the home ended. It was spectacular! As I opened the car door, Annie appeared on her porch, greeting us with a friendly wave. We climbed the stairs and she invited us inside.

Leading us past a refrigerator covered with a lifetime's worth of photos of children, grandchildren, and sailing, I lingered there to study them. Annie took us to her sunroom so that we could "get our bearings." The room was completely made of glass, and everything in the room was white. The bright sun hurt my eyes. It was like a glimpse into heaven, or, better yet, a Windex commercial. It was an amazing view looking down from their lofty house on the edge of a cliff. Peering out through the trees, one could take in a picturesque blue sky and the sparkling water of a wide river below. She pointed out the bridge we had just crossed, the way to Lake Ontario, and the yacht club across the river where she and her husband, Eugene, were members. Then, leading us back to the kitchen, she positioned herself on a stool and offered us chairs around a table facing her. Eugene sat off to the side in "his" chair, where he would be more of a witness to the event than a participant. This was her time to be the center of attention; he played the role of supportive husband perfectly. Her high stool was not one of superiority but of a mother tending her brood or a lifeguard at a beach, ever watchful for someone in need. She only sat for a brief moment before she got back up to play hostess.

"First things first," she said, while serving mini blueberry muffins and chocolate macaroons. "Can I get you some juice? If you want coffee, you're out of luck." Her playful smile put everyone in the room at ease. I reached for a macaroon to be polite, took a bite, and then reached for a second one at the request of my taste buds. Settling back on her perch, she asked the first question, "How did you find me?"

I launched into the story of how she was first mentioned in Dan's journal, how everyone wanted to sail on Annie's boat, and how Rick Rhoads, son of the camp director, had helped with her last name. That led me to her MIT-graduate commodore father, her sisters, her daughter (an accomplished sailor), and finally to Annie herself. I gave her a gift bag with several old newspaper clippings of her family history I'd located on the Internet. She was tickled to have them to share with her sisters and grandchildren. Her eyes widened when she also found a Burleigh Hill Sailing Camp hat inside. With a huge grin, she placed it on her head and announced to Eugene that she was in charge. I could tell she was pleased, and he was amused.

SNOW ANGELS ON THE MOON

Memories of Burleigh Hill took over the conversation. She brought out nautical charts and spread them out on the table. Each one had hand-written notes logging the places she'd visited and routes she'd taken.

She reminisced about overnight camping on Pemaquid Beach and waking up to find her boat missing from the cove. How would she explain that to camp director Lester Rhoads? Somehow the shackle had come loose on the anchor and the boat had washed ashore unharmed on the sandy beach. She dove into the water and made several attempts to retrieve the anchor. Finally, she came up with it, and they all managed to put the boat back in the water. Much like the saying about Las Vegas, she hoped that what had happened on Pemaquid Beach would stay on Pemaquid Beach.

She explained that the camp was more than just a sailing camp. No one was forced to do anything. Some people never even got near a sailboat. Their weeks at Burleigh Hill were filled with whatever they wanted to do. But having said that, she noted that the camp excelled in teaching sailing. At the beginning of summer, the kids came into camp, and eight weeks later, most of them came out as sailors.

On the day of the rescue, some of the boat captains had wanted to stay in Camden for one more day until the weather passed. Many parents, however, would soon be arriving in Boothbay to pick up their children. The camp director said they had a schedule to keep and didn't want to disappoint the parents. Despite protests, the five sailboats and one powerboat headed for Tenants Harbor.

Annie said there was no question they were in rough weather that kept building throughout the day. It presented a challenge to *all* the boats, not just the *Debby*. Each one of the captains had their hands full, and two other boats had to be towed to safety that day, as well. Annie recalled that she herself had broken some batting on the sail and was pretty relieved to reach Tenants Harbor that afternoon. It was a day of tough sailing.

As I told of my discoveries, Annie was pleased to hear that the kids remembered her with fondness. Her recollection of Susan Cheever was that she was a cutie, and Leslie Lewis was sweet but very street-smart. Annie was at Burleigh Hill for both the summers of '57 and '58.

ON HOLD

When the time came to leave, Annie's hospitality did not stop at her property line. Wanting to get us heading in the right direction, Eugene and Annie had us follow them to Lake Ontario, where we stopped to take group pictures. Thanking them both, we parted ways. As I pulled onto the highway I couldn't have concurred with Dan's journal more; I could now see why everyone wanted to be on "Annie's boat."

We made our way down the Finger Lakes with a new purpose in mind. It just so happened that we would be passing by someone else who had been a fixture at the camp at the time of the rescue: Joane. In 1958, she had just graduated from college and was working as a cook at Burleigh Hill. Eventually, she and Lester (twenty years her senior) had a May/September romance that saw them married the following year. By the mid-1960s, the marriage was over, though, and they went their separate ways. Could she still be connected to Leslie? It was a question I needed to ask.

Through my research, I'd found out she had remarried and was living in Upstate New York. Her husband was a college professor, and she was running an herb shop. My several attempts at contacting them had gone unanswered. Apparently, I had an old address, but as long as I was in the neighborhood, I had to investigate.

Finding their home was proving to be nearly impossible—no house number, no mailbox, and no house. And looking for her orchid and herb shop that was said to be located in a hollow wasn't any easier, either.

After several trips down into the hollow and back out, we decided to forget the whole thing. She was not expecting us, and if she had never received my e-mails or letters, would have no idea of her importance to us. I would need to go to her door in a cold call and explain who I was and the purpose of our visit. Normally, I run in the other direction when faced with such a situation.

On our final pass out of the hollow, we saw a lady with a walking stick sauntering up the road. She smiled. We stopped. Could this be Joane? Nope, it wasn't, and the lady had never heard of her. However, she did know the whereabouts of an herb shop that used to be a hundred yards down the road. In fact, it was her neighbor. Strange,

153

though; she didn't know her neighbor's name. Not the friendliest of hollows, I thought to myself.

We thanked the woman and with a little glimmer of hope turned back around. It was getting late in the afternoon as we entered the driveway described by the woman on the road. The treetops all but blotted out the sky, blocking most of what sunlight was left of the day. Continuing down the dirt road, it looked as if it dead-ended at a bunch of trees. However, when we got down in there, the road turned sharply left, then to the right. As I maneuvered our vehicle, I noticed in my rearview mirror that the trees seemed to close behind us like a door. I couldn't help but feel like I was trapped somehow.

Slowly passing a greenhouse that obviously was out of business, we were disappointed. It would have been a friendly icebreaker to stop and buy some herbs. We parked facing their house. I questioned whether this was such a good idea after all. If I had followed my instincts, I would've put the car in reverse, backed out the entire length of the road, and forgotten the whole thing. But we had come this far. I couldn't turn back now, for I would always have the question in my mind about leaving that one stone unturned.

I am not sure what I said to convince my feet to get out of the car and proceed toward the steps that afternoon, but it worked. My heart pounded as a shadow appeared at the window blocking the lone light in the house. Oh, good, I thought to myself, someone's home. The voice in my head cracked a bit as I slowly ascended the steps. The door to the house opened and a white-haired gentleman in shorts and a bright yellow T-shirt walked toward us. He met us halfway down the stairs with half a smile. I was relieved.

"Are you Dan?" I asked.

He nodded, "Yes, I am."

"My name is Russ Lane, and this is my wife, Heidi. We're from Maine."

"Ooookay," he said in a prolonged pronunciation of the word, which, in translation, meant *And I care about that because...?*

I took a deep breath and started to explain about my dad, the rescue, and that we were looking for Joane. He listened politely as I stammered over a word here and there. Heidi stood behind me and off to the side in a show of support. The place didn't seem so scary anymore.

As I finished, he said, "Oh, you want my wife. And it's pronounced *Jo-Ann*" he corrected. He turned around and yelled up to the house, "Jo-Ann, Burleigh Hill has reared its ugly head again!"

Did he say *ugly? Again?* Something told me my gift bag containing a hat and pictures of Burleigh Hill would not be well received.

There was no doubt in my mind that the woman who let the screen door slam behind her as she came down the steps was Joane. She carefully navigated each step of the crooked stairway, her movements not those of vulnerability but of superiority. She continued her methodical descent with the intent to always maintain higher ground. I tried to force a smile so she would not see me as a threat. Her husband excused himself saying they were late getting ready to attend some volunteer function.

"What do you want?" she asked sternly.

"I am trying to get my father recognition for a rescue that happened in 1958 with kids from Burleigh Hill. We're just looking for some information. Here's a newspaper article telling about the rescue." I reached out, showing it to her. She didn't look down at the page.

"Why would your father need to rescue anybody? We had our *own* powerboat. Those kids were never in the water, maybe a little water up to their ankles in the boat. No one was in any danger that day. Those kids exaggerated; all kids exaggerate."

It was clear that no matter what I said, her recollections of the day were set in stone. Was she possibly parroting what her first husband might have told her?

"Sorry to bother you," I apologized as I started my retreat. "Would you like a picture of the campers?" She stretched her neck to see the picture.

"I'm not even in that," she scolded.

"Isn't that you?" Heidi stepped between us in an effort not to lose any ground and show a little defiance herself.

"Yes, that's me," Joane had to agree, but you could tell she didn't want to acknowledge the fact.

SNOW ANGELS ON THE MOON

"Do you want this picture?" I offered again.

"I have all that stuff," she snarled.

"So, were you a cook at the camp?" Heidi asked in her normal cheery voice, trying to keep the conversation light.

"Me? A cook? NO! Certainly not!" She looked disgusted at the accusation. "I was the camp *dietician*," she proclaimed. Her posture seemed to take on a prideful attitude. (I was relieved that Heidi did not raise the fact that to some of the campers she had been known as the "salad girl.")

"About this rescue." Joane looked down her nose at us. "Did you ask the director? He would have the information you are looking for, if anyone would. But he's probably dead."

"Yes, I believe he passed away in 2001," I answered, looking for an opportunity to turn and run. We'd only been there for a few minutes before I began to wonder what had happened to the sun. Darkness must come early to the hollow...or perhaps it never leaves.

"I was married to him, you know. He was my first husband," she offered, looking straight at Heidi.

"Oh, were you married long?" Heidi asked, already knowing the answer.

Joane's face tightened and her lips puckered, evidently at the foul taste the thought of her marriage left in her mouth. She did not answer. The kindly white-haired gentleman returned, explaining that he was sorry, but they had to leave. "I have nothing more to offer," Joane said as she backed up the steps, facing us all the while.

"We apologize for bothering you," I said one last time. I had forgotten all about asking whether she had kept in touch with Leslie, but I guess the answer was obvious. Her days at Burleigh Hill must not have been kind ones.

"I hope you find what you're looking for." Joane's husband's words were sincere. "Back up onto the grass by the greenhouse. It's a lot easier to get out the driveway from there."

Thanking him, I jumped into our car and followed his instructions to the letter. I never looked back. The trees parted in front of us, allowing us to go, and I am certain I heard the rustle of the leaves as they snapped shut behind us.

156

ON HOLD

That afternoon had not turned out the way I had expected. I had come bearing gifts in exchange for a little information. It was one stone that might better have been left unturned. At least now it wouldn't be an unanswered question to haunt me later on.

CHAPTER 22

A PLACE ONCE CALLED HOME

It didn't seem possible that two weeks had come and gone since Heidi's and my adventure in Upstate New York. Now I was off on another one, and I was happy to be taking my parents along with me. We were heading back to Whitehead Island.

If you had told me two months ago that Dad would be up for such an excursion, I never would have believed it. He could barely walk some days. However, when the possibility of a trip to the island arose, he declared he was ready. Who was I to argue? After contacting Gigi and Matt, I was grateful that they were willing to do whatever it took to bring Dad back to the island after all these years.

I have Susan Cheever to thank for the entire opportunity. She had done some investigating on various lighthouse websites, but had found nothing about the rescue, nor about my father, on their keeper list. In order to rectify that, she got in touch with some of the webmasters and told them about my father. One lighthouse historian, Jeremy D'Entremont, took an interest and added the rescue story to his site. He invited us out to Whitehead Island to show my video to a group of lighthouse enthusiasts on a weekend retreat. We jumped at the chance.

The heavy mist gave way to a driving rain as I pulled into my parents' dooryard. I sat there hoping it would ease up before I ran into the house to get my father and mother. It was going to be a long day for them, and we didn't need anyone getting wet before we even started. That was a good plan in theory, but Dad seemed to have other ideas.

The rain was too much for the windshield wipers to handle on intermittent. A half second of visibility was replaced by two seconds

SNOW ANGELS ON THE MOON

of blurriness. With one swipe of the blade, I saw Dad looking out the front door. Thus began a series of snapshots. The door opened. Swipe. He is at the top of the ramp. Swipe. He's halfway down the ramp. So much for keeping him (and me) dry. Quickly, I jumped out and ran to offer him a hand. Thankfully, he used the railing that went the length of the garage to steady himself. Without it, he could be like a runaway train, ending up derailed in front of my car. That's all we would've needed this morning. But who could fault him? It had been a long time since I had seen him so eager to come along on a trip with me. Helping him to the passenger-side seat (without incident), I noticed something was missing.

"Dad? Where's your cane?"

"Must be back in the house. Gee, how did I forget that?" He was all smiles. Dad reached to buckle his seat belt. Obviously, he was prouder of getting to the car without his cane than concerned about the fact that he might have forgotten it.

"I'd say someone's excited!" I exclaimed, closing the passenger door and dashing to the house. I found his cane on the counter and my mother heading for the door with her arms full. Taking half of her load, I turned and, like a relay race, took it to the car. The rain was turning back into a light mist. My mother had followed me out, and soon we were all safe, somewhat dry, and heading up U.S. Route 1.

The rain had stopped and started several times on our way to Spruce Head. We parked facing the ocean so we could stay warm and cozy while keeping a lookout for the boat that would be coming for us. Off in the distance, a speck was growing larger by the minute. I told my parents that Whitehead Light Station had a nice boat with deck chairs and a roof that would keep them dry and warm and out of the wind.

Mother and I got out of the car and walked to the end of the dock. She had never been much of a storyteller, but that's not because she didn't have a story to tell. I just think she never wanted to draw the attention away from Dad and his stories. Looking out at the harbor full of boats, she took advantage of Dad's absence and started to reminisce on her own. They were stories I had never heard before that day. She talked about being out on the island alone with the wife of another

160

lightkeeper. He had been sick in the hospital and Dad had to take the boat to Spruce Head to bring him back to the island. Darkness and fog came in like they were joined at the hip.

Mother said that when they'd first gotten to the island, Dad had shown her how to operate the light and the foghorn. It was a quick lesson because the odds were she would never have to do it. However, there she was, months later, in that very situation. Struggling to remember the process, the wives finally figured out the foghorn and the light in the tower and Whitehead Light Station was up and running.

Meanwhile, the husbands were inching their way across the bay in a leaky boat with an engine that liked to stall at the most inopportune times. It was the thickest fog that either of them had ever encountered, and the darkness made it ten times worse. Dad was bent over at the bow looking down with the flashlight hovering over the water, while the other lightkeeper at the helm was watching their heading on the compass. Too much one way and they would miss the island and end up somewhere in the middle of the Atlantic. Too much the other direction and they would run aground and poke a hole in the boat on one of the many dangerous ledges. Approaching the island on the back side, the trees obscured the light in the tower. As Dad searched the water for ledges, all of a sudden he heard the foghorn cut through the darkness, calling him home. "That a girl, Sandra." Dad praised her name to the waves as the foghorn helped guide them the rest of the way. Mother said it was a dark and scary night and remembered that the sweetest sound was the slam of the front door when Dad finally got home.

As I watched my mother tell her story, the years slipped off her face and she was twenty years old again. I wondered what other gems she had hidden away.

Hearing an approaching outboard brought us back to 2015. The speck that had appeared earlier off in the distance had grown into a boat. Unfortunately, it was not the boat from Whitehead. This was a smaller boat, a Boston Whaler with an open cockpit. False alarm. Looking back toward the ocean, I wondered if they were running late. I didn't have the wrong day, did I? The boat pulled alongside the float and, as if on cue, the rain started. The figure who reached down to tie up both

SNOW ANGELS ON THE MOON

ends of the boat looked a little too familiar. It was Captain "Welcome" Matt, and his hand waved a greeting in one direction and beckoned us down in the other. Mother and I went to get Dad and our bags.

Opening the car door, I briefed Dad on the situation. "Uh-oh, change of plans. Prepare to get wet!"

"No problem, I've been wet before," was Dad's reply with a smile. Not the answer I was expecting, but it sounded like my dad from years before.

We began our descent down the ramp. Matt was busy clearing away the bow area and started wiping the water from the front seat. I steadied my father, and we eased our way down onto the float, taking baby steps so as not to slip on the wet dock. I could see Matt wasn't gaining much ground over wiping the seat from the falling rain. The boat shifted from side to side as Matt walked over to help with Dad. It seemed a bit more tipsy compared to the bigger boat they'd used last time.

"This is gonna be fun," I whispered in Dad's ear, trying to hide a worried tone. I must not have done a very good job concealing my concern because Dad started to console me.

"Oh, we'll get aboard her okay. I might not get back out, but we'll get aboard her." His tone was one of eagerness and excitement.

Matt met us on the float, explaining that the bigger boat had engine trouble, and he had to borrow this one. He apologized that we might get a little wet.

"No problem. We've been wet before," I said, adopting both my father's words and tone.

I'm not sure how we did it, but we got Dad aboard and seated in the bow without anyone ending up in the water. Soon we were skipping our way across the waves with my mother and father feeling the brunt of the wind and rain. It was safe to say by the look on their faces, they were having the time of their lives, taking turns smiling and pointing things out to each other. You could see the memories come alive as their eyes sparkled with excitement. They were more than being transported to the island; they were being transported back sixty years, to a moment in time when they were a young married couple on the adventure of a lifetime.

162

A PLACE ONCE CALLED HOME

Of course, the rain stopped as we approached the island. Almost miraculously, Dad's balance was better, and he had more of a spring in his step. He pretty much got out of the boat and climbed aboard the John Deere four-wheeler on his own.

First stop: the boathouse. Dad and Mother walked inside, and the memories started to flow. With Matt as a new audience, Dad talked of how they'd been stuck on the island without a boat.

Back on the four-wheeler, Matt took Dad off into the woods on a joyride. Mother and I walked the road to the other side of the island. The pathway was like an old friend leading her back home. When we came into the clearing, there stood Whitehead Light Station. A smile appeared on my mother's face that never left for the rest of the day. Matt drove Dad up to the lighthouse and parked. From that vantage point, Dad could see everything, but he still opted to get off the four-wheeler and stand on his own two feet looking out over the horizon. He looked strong and full of life.

People appeared and came up to us to introduce themselves. They were lighthouse enthusiasts who were spending the weekend as guests of Whitehead Light Station. Some of the women attached themselves to my mother, offering her hugs and asking her questions.

No one noticed someone appearing out of the woods until we heard a voice from behind. The voice was unmistakably that of David Gamage. Dad's face lit up with delight. Then the stories really started to flow! Standing between David Gamage and my father, I could not help but think about how humble these two men were. Maybe that's what being a true hero is all about.

Soon we made our way down to the whistle house, which was set up with rows of seats and a movie screen. The entire island was invited, not just those attending the lighthouse retreat. The staff and the Swan family, whose summer home was on the far side of the island, were welcomed as well.

Jeremy D'Entremont, lighthouse historian and emcee for the event, introduced us to the audience and it was show time. It was the first time that I got to sit in a room full of people I did not know and observe their reactions to the story. It was satisfying for me to hear the emotion

163

the video drew from the crowd. There was some laughter and quite a few tears in the room during the viewing. They gave Dad, Mom, and David a standing ovation at the end. It was a very moving experience for us all. A question-and-answer session followed. The three heroes were like celebrities as they all posed for pictures. (I even managed to get into a couple of them myself.) Jeremy presented us a book that he'd authored on lighthouses of Penobscot Bay, which includes Whitehead.

We had more than enough volunteers to help Dad get up the stairs that led into the lighthouse. He grabbed the first chair he came to and folks came in to mingle while they talked to him as though it were an open house event. My mother walked through the entire house, both upstairs and down, sorting out her memories and answering questions as to how the house had changed. She seemed to have an entourage everywhere she went.

We had a full room around the dining table at lunch. The sixteen of us were quite cozy, but no one minded. By now, everyone knew everyone else. The magic of Whitehead Island had happened again!

After an afternoon of stories and making new friends, I could tell Dad didn't want to leave. It was a feeling I could well relate to from my last visit to the island. But we loaded Dad back into the John Deere, and Mother and I hit the trail. It was high tide when we got back to the dock, which made it easier for Dad to board the boat. It would've been easy no matter what because he wasn't just walking down the ramp: He was walking on cloud nine.

As we cast off from the dock, Matt slowly idled away from the shore. Looking back at the shrinking island, we noticed someone emerge from one of the cottages. The person made their way down onto the shoreline and stood there for a moment. Then, standing on tippy-toes, the figure made big sweeping motions over his head with his arms. It was David Gamage waving goodbye.

On the ride back to Spruce Head, I fought to keep my balance standing in the back of the Boston Whaler. That was probably a good thing. Otherwise the low drone of the outboard would have certainly lulled me to sleep. It had been a long day, but it had been a great day! The old memories that had surfaced from my parents during the trip were

A PLACE ONCE CALLED HOME

amazing, and I was so very thankful for the new ones created after having met so many wonderful people. Watching my parents seated at the bow with their heads resting against each other, I knew they had to be tired, too. But it was a good tired, a grateful tired, that had brought them back to the place they'd once called home—Whitehead Island.

CHAPTER 23

THE UNREST OF THE STORY

The conversation on the ride home surprised me. I thought my parents would be exhausted from the day's events, but it was quite the opposite. Dad talked a blue streak while Mother waited for him to take a breath. When she saw an opening, she would quickly interject one of her own many highlights from the afternoon and sigh, remarking, "What a wonderful day this has been." I kept smiling and taking it all in; I wondered how long the magic of Whitehead Island would last.

My parents were animated, and Dad was so positive. It was a side of Dad that I was seeing more and more of after uncovering the rescue story. As a younger man, he had been a good father and a hard worker, but, to be honest, some days he seemed like a glass-half-empty sort of guy. He had a good memory for everything bad that had ever happened to him. I had always written that off as a result of the lack of nurturing from being raised in such a large family. However, later I began to realize it must have stemmed from something deeper, more sinister than that.

It was something that we never talked about within the family growing up, but we sure did experience it. Most of the time, Dad was an all-around good guy. However, every so often, he would battle his "demons," as he called it. It would come out in short bouts of intense anger, long periods of depression, and continual low—almost nonexistent—self-esteem.

The worst of these experiences happened on the water. One particularly bad day lobstering—I was probably nine or ten—we were missing traps, the catch was down, and, at one point, we ended up on a ledge. Dad became extremely angry. I kept my distance and retreated to the stern of the boat. Violently shaking, he cursed God for the day

SNOW ANGELS ON THE MOON

he was born. Grabbing the knife from the dashboard, he yelled out to the heavens for enough courage to plunge it into his chest. Afraid of what I was about to witness, I cowered in the corner, praying that God would make everything okay. Somehow the situation was defused, and things did get better. I am grateful to this day that God answered the whispered prayer of a little boy over his father's anguished pleading. From that time on, whenever I climbed aboard the boat, I would head straight for the helm, grab the knife from the dashboard, and hide it in the bait barrel. It was for Dad's sake, not mine. My own safety never felt threatened.

It was always a mystery to me. What could cause such rage and outbursts from this otherwise good man? I wondered if it was a dislike of being on the ocean. If it was, I felt sorry for Dad, for it would be a hard place for him to avoid, considering he had spent most of his life on the water. The ocean had been so much of his past; he knew of nothing else to count on for his future. But it wasn't just the ocean that was the problem. I started to see another common thread to these rare but all too real episodes.

During my own youth, my body seemed to be racing toward maturity and leaving my brain in the dust. (It has been playing catch-up ever since.) The result was that I was a clumsy and uncoordinated kid. My parents called me "accident-prone." That's probably a nice way to put it, but I was always in need of stitches or having to have something put into a cast.

Whenever I had the misfortune of getting hurt, Dad's automatic response was anger. One would expect that a typical reaction from someone who loved you would be of concern and compassion. More than once, I remember being raced to the hospital with Dad cursing that I was ruined for life. When we arrived, Mother would rush me inside while Dad stayed out in the car, refusing to come in. I learned to hide my injuries from my father for as long as possible—or, better yet, not tell him at all. The expression "playing through the pain" had become part of everything I did during those clumsy years.

We never brought up the subject of Dad's days in the military. If *he* did, that was okay. But we didn't. He always told me that the first time he ever saw me, *he* was on leave from the Coast Guard. He had just arrived from Boston, and for some reason, we met in a shoe store in Damariscotta. It was about a week after I was born, and he remembers me being the homeliest thing he ever saw.

It was confusing. Why wasn't he there when I was born? It was not until later in life that I found out he was in a hospital himself down in Boston. Eventually he ended up on Staten Island at another hospital, where he was confined for three months before he was honorably discharged from the Coast Guard and sent back home.

After suffering in silence for years, finally he was diagnosed with Post Traumatic Stress Disorder (PTSD) in the 1990s and was getting some much-needed help from the Veterans Administration. The anger issues somewhat subsided, but Dad continued to battle with bouts of depression and a feeling that his life was a failure. His depression influenced my decision to search for the five people he had once saved. While I could never convince him of the fact that his life had value, it was my hope that maybe they could. Then, later, it was at a showing of the movie that someone commented, "Your dad must have survivor's guilt." This was a new term to me at the time, but one that made perfect sense.

During five years in the Coast Guard, he was on eight different lighthouses. Two were on the mainland, five were on islands, and one was a "spark plug" light just standing out of the water. Not all light stations were like Whitehead, a place where he could bring his family. The other lighthouses made the job of lightkeeper a difficult one—places like Mark Island, where he would consistently be abandoned to face loneliness and isolation for weeks at a time. Combine that with the mundane and repetitive task of tending the light, and you have fertile ground for PTSD to bury itself even deeper into one's psyche.

Dad tells one story of being alone out on Mark Island. He could smell a storm brewing in the air. By nightfall, the waves were at full force, as they almost reached the steps leading up into the lighthouse. Automated like the light, he would wake up every hour to check on the light and then struggle to go back to sleep. It was a little past midnight and he lay in the dark listening to the howling wind and driving rain trying

SNOW ANGELS ON THE MOON

to find its way into every possible crack and crevice. Just as sleep was about to come once again, he heard a noise at the bottom of the stairs that demanded his attention. Was that a footstep? Bolting upright in bed, he strained to hear. The confirmation of another footstep set his heart racing. In a slow, deliberate climb he heard someone ascending the staircase... Who else could be on this island? There were no other houses. And the storm was too fierce for anyone to venture out by boat on purpose. The footsteps grew louder until they reached the landing, and then started toward his room. Reaching down by the side of his bed, he quietly brought his shotgun to his lap. As the last footstep stopped right outside his bedroom, he lifted the barrel of the gun and aimed it at the door.

He waited for what seemed like an eternity. Gathering up enough courage to slip out of bed, he made his way to the door. When he opened it, he found nothing. He searched the house, then went down to the water to check on the boathouse. Nothing seemed out of place. Running back to the house, he almost didn't want to go back inside for fear of what might be waiting for him.

Was his mind playing tricks on him, or was it a ghostly visitor? Neither explanation gave him comfort. He didn't get much sleep the rest of that night, but somehow, he made peace with the torture of having to spend even more nights alone on Mark Island.

Years later, after my father had long been out of the Coast Guard, my mother would wake to find him clawing at the walls of their bedroom. Dad had awoken to a lightkeeper's nightmare, the horror of darkness. Thinking the light was out in the tower and passing ships could be in danger, he was trying to climb the tower to light the light. His sense of duty and "not on my watch" mentality had carried on through the years along with his PTSD.

Suddenly, it all made sense: watching his best friend die and the survivor's guilt he must have suffered for all the years that followed; then facing the need to venture out into yet another storm with the potential of seeing five more people die—unless he could act fast enough. Would the horror of seeing Billy L'Heureux being swept away before his eyes be repeated five times over? Now, learning of the

170

prolonged isolation and the frightening situations he had endured at other Maine lighthouses—a difficult burden to carry for all those years—it was no wonder the "demons" had such a deep-rooted hold on Dad!

My thoughts returned to the five campers in the water and their near-death experience. For some, the memory may have been worse than for others. They had been scooped up that afternoon and were back in their bunks at Boothbay later that night. No one was taken to a hospital to be checked out. There was no conversation or debriefing to see how everyone was doing. The incident was swept under the rug as far as Burleigh Hill Camp was concerned. Surely, it would not be good for business if word leaked out. The daily newspaper was no longer made available to the campers or their parents, who had arrived to pick up the kids. The article in the *Portland Press Herald* would have largely gone unnoticed anyway, as it was hidden under the headline "Two Beaches Closed by Tide, Surf."

Without any support, those five teens had been abandoned to fend for themselves in dealing with the terror of facing death. Susan Cheever reported that for the first few nights after I had contacted her, she woke up with feelings she probably should have processed fifty-seven years earlier. My own near-death experience in the canoe had given me a few restless nights, too.

As I helped steady Dad up the ramp to his house, I realized he was even more of a hero than when we had left that morning. Undiagnosed and going it alone for years must have been an enormous challenge. It caused me to wonder how many others are out there battling an unknown enemy as they suffer in silence day after day.

CHAPTER 24

WHERE THE MAGIC HAPPENS

Waking up way too early the next morning, my mind refused to roll over and go back to sleep. The experience of taking my parents to Whitehead the day before would forever be etched in my memory. The sights, the sounds, the smells were a lot to process, and I knew it would all take time. I just didn't expect my mind to have me up at "zero dark thirty" as it churned away. I thought my brain would have better sense than that. Come to think of it, being my second visit to the island in less than three months, shouldn't I already have Whitehead mostly figured out? Then it hit me: It wasn't just the island but the ever-changing parade of people that had my mind working overtime. They were what kept the magic alive on Whitehead Island.

And of course, there was the so-called world premiere of my film *Looking for a Hero* to think about. It had been wonderful and yet agonizing at the same time. Seeing the crowd react as a whole, first laughing then crying, told me that the film had done its job in connecting with the audience. But was I happy with the finished product? Not really. Some parts were painful to watch as the flaws of the film rose to the surface. The audience didn't appear to notice, but I sure did. Like the lessons I learned working with Dad over the years, I knew I had to go back and fix the cinematic mistakes, if only for my own peace of mind.

The enthusiasm of the crowd with the rolling of the credits and during the Q&A afterwards only whetted my appetite to tell the story more completely. The ten-minute video I was once so proud of now seemed lacking. The story didn't end the day after the rescue, so why did the movie? It was still alive and happening today. I know it's been said that you should always leave the audience wanting a little more.

SNOW ANGELS ON THE MOON

But I left them in the middle of the meal—no dessert, no coffee after-wards. Even though I wanted to jump in with both feet and fix things, I knew time would be better spent reflecting on what I had done so far and seeing how to better tell the story.

In the meantime, I had a nagging feeling there was one more stone that I had not completely turned over: that of captain and counselor, Peter Laylin. The experience of meeting Susan, Dan, and Jeff face-to-face and hearing their story was as magical as being out on Whitehead. I felt a need to do the same with Peter. However, I did have one obsta-cle. My travels in pursuit of the rescue story had put a bit of a drain on my finances for the year, and one more trip didn't appear to be in the cards. I began pleading with myself to rationalize the expense. Heidi hadn't seen Drew in a while; we could go visit him in LA, then rent a car and drive to Tucson. It could be our next year's Christmas and birthday presents all rolled up into one. Down deep, I knew no matter what the cost, it was an investment that I needed to make not just in the story, but in myself if I was ever going to be a writer. I was torn. Then, waking up one night, I could hear the cacti calling my name and I knew what I had to do. In the morning, I announced to Heidi, "We're going to Arizona!"

November soon arrived, and after spending a few days in Los Ange-les visiting our son, we picked up our rent-a-car and hit the wide-open dusty trail to Arizona. The contrast to my home state of Maine was huge. But I must admit, as an Old Salt from Down East plunked down in the Old West, I kind of liked it. Maine can be wet and humid no matter what the season, while Arizona remains hot and dry as a bone. Which, I might add, felt good on my body and seemed to help my Parkinson's. The only thing dry about Maine is its humor.

Upon arrival in Tucson, we drove by acres and acres of airplanes preserved and stored at the ready. I had always heard this was the ideal place for such a thing. It got me thinking about how this climate must preserve people, too. Everyone we saw looked young. Add a little hair coloring and I could see sixty becoming the new forty pretty easily. Just like airplanes and people, I thought, maybe I should think about putting myself into winter storage down here as well.

WHERE THE MAGIC HAPPENS

Having to spend two nights in Tucson, I was torn again. A high school classmate, Ruth, who had moved out west, heard that we were visiting the area. She offered to let us stay with her and her husband, Mitch. However, my Parkinson's had become more difficult to hide. And with my sleep habits having me up all hours of the night, I thought a hotel might be a less obtrusive option for everyone involved. Ruth wouldn't take no for an answer, so we gratefully accepted their hospitality.

After a late night of talking about our high school days, Ruth made us a hearty breakfast and we were off to the PIMA Air and Space Museum. Peter Laylin was a docent there and as part of our visit offered to give us a tour. As a lover of all things aviation, I was more than a little excited. Right on schedule, Peter greeted us and escorted us inside. Knowing we had a lot of ground to cover, he switched directly into tour-guide mode. It was as if his aviation training had taken over. Like the perfect combination of pilot and docent, Peter had a checklist that he was following to keep us on track. Strangely, though, we hardly discussed the main reason we had come: to find out about Burleigh Hill and the rescue. However, when we happened upon any of Peter's coworkers, he introduced us and explained how my father had saved his life.

When it came time for lunch, we retreated out of the desert sun to the museum's cafeteria-style restaurant called the Flight Grill. Peter took off his docent hat and set it in the chair beside him. It was as if the hat had shifted his gears, as the conversation immediately turned to his experience as a counselor at Burleigh Hill.

In 1957, Peter, a student at Colby College, had been looking for a summer job. Lester Rhoads, in need of camp counselors, put ads in several local college newspapers. Peter applied for a position. The only problem was that Burleigh Hill was a sailing camp and, admittedly, he was pretty green as a sailor. But Lester hired him anyway. Raised in the Midwest, Peter and the ocean were not that familiar with each other. In fact, his main task as a counselor was to oversee a rifle for one young camper. His orders were to follow this kid around and let him shoot the rifle whenever he wanted. That's a scenario I could never imagine happening today, but those were very different times. Also, I wasn't sure if they pandered to all the campers that way, but something tells

175

me Lester was pretty accommodating for the right price. It was apparent that whatever Peter lacked in sailing skills, he must have more than made up for in integrity. Even back in those days, you did not give the responsibility of a gun to just anybody.

When the conversation turned to the incident at Whitehead, Peter took on a more serious tone. He remembered being in the water and clinging to the *Debby's* bow. With every minute that passed, the gravity of the situation sank in deeper. Hopelessness followed by a feeling of total sadness blanketed him. He was sorry he would never get to see his mother and father again. He had resigned himself to the fact that death was inevitable. Then a boat on the horizon appeared like an angel and they were saved.

We ate the last few bites of our lunch and Peter put his docent hat back on. Like the flip of a switch, Peter the camp counselor became Peter the tour guide once again. Back outside, he explained that this was the first time he had led a tour through the entire museum. Normally, the docents have certain sections they are responsible for. It was obvious that Peter's vast knowledge of aviation showed that he was more than up for the task.

Making our way back outside, we were greeted by a stiff afternoon breeze like a blast from a hot-air furnace. We turned the corner, and there, amongst a row of large transport aircraft, was the one airplane I had been waiting to see, the C-124 Globemaster II. As we approached the plane, Peter's eyes had an extra hint of sparkle as he explained this was what he'd flown in and out of Southeast Asia during the early 1960s. Standing next to the huge landing gear, my tour guide transformed before my eyes into a lieutenant fresh out of flight school. It wasn't difficult to picture Peter as a young pilot kicking the tires on his preflight as the troops loaded into the airplane. I walked along the fuselage and was astonished by its girth, which I could only describe as "beefy," a term seldom used in the sleek, streamlined world of aeronautics. It was a technological beast that would keep the most conscientious pilot busy with complicated mechanical systems and four huge radial engines. Each engine had twenty-eight cylinders that turned a massive propeller. It was easy to tell why she was nicknamed "Old

WHERE THE MAGIC HAPPENS

Shaky." It was a noisy, rough ride for the passengers, but still a sweet one for those heading home from a war zone.

These were giant machines from the bygone days of aviation that required a separate flight engineer just to monitor all the systems. Peter explained that the airplane was already obsolete by the time he flew it, but it had enabled him to see a lot of the world and kept him safely out of active combat zones when flying in and through Vietnam.

As the afternoon came to an end, I was so very glad that I traveled this far to meet Peter. He had come a long way from being a college student answering a want ad in a campus newspaper.

They say any landing a pilot can walk away from is a good landing. In an unforgiving sky, I suppose that is true. And shaking Peter's hand as we parted, I couldn't help but think that must apply to sailboats, too.

CHAPTER 25

FROZEN

New Year's Day can often be a letdown for those of us who live in Maine. Not only do the holidays come to an end, but all we have to look forward to is long stretches of time cut into chunks with endearing names like the "dead of winter" and "mud season." Maybe the bears have it right when they choose to hibernate until spring. But sleeping your life away doesn't seem like the best solution, either.

Looking out my office window, I saw less of the world each day. The ice and snow kept building up little by little on each pane until it was like looking through the porthole of a ship. Am I stuck on this voyage until springtime? I both feared and hoped for the same answer of yes.

These winter months on the calendar are the perfect time to get lost in a project. In the name of research, I was forced to review tons of video to see what would make the cut in my film. However, being able to see the luscious green grass, deep blue ocean, and white cotton-candy clouds floating by on a canvas of baby-blue sky was just the medicine to help escape a cold dark winter's night. It was the perfect summer, captured on film. I would turn on the surround sound, close my eyes, and lie in bed listening in the dark. Such gems as the crunching sound of walking in the woods on Whitehead Island, hearing the birds singing in the trees, and riding with the wind as it whistled through the rigging of the sails were all soothing to my ears. It took me back to the day in July when I'd gotten to sail for real.

Cindy is a good friend. Better still, she is a good friend with a sailboat. After hearing about the rescue story and my project, she offered to take me on her boat to do some filming. What an opportunity! *Pearl*, her eighteen-foot sailboat, was similar to those used at Burleigh Hill

SNOW ANGELS ON THE MOON

Camp. As an added bonus, Cindy can put on a Long Island accent to sound just like most of the campers probably did back in the day. But, if the truth be known, her accent is not actually put on. She comes by it naturally. (If anyone asks about her being "from away," though, you didn't hear it from me.)

The sound of the outboard was reassuring when we motored out of Pemaquid that summer day. Leaving the mouth of the harbor, we passed by Noses Rock; at least that's what Dad had always called it. I never questioned him. It seemed logical to me that the nose would be located somewhere around the mouth. It was not until I was older that I noticed it on a chart. It was labeled "Knowles Rocks." What a shocker! All the fishermen called it "Noses," so I thought that was the correct name. Of course, the one common thread in the discrepancy was my ears. Maybe they were saying it right, and I was hearing it wrong. Could I have been the problem all along? Oh, no, that's foolishness, but it did get me thinking. There is a difference between storytelling with a bunch of fishermen and documenting an event in film or in writing. You should be sure and accurate when the story is to be repeated beyond the end of the dock.

As Cindy shut down the motor, it was hard for me to hear the silence of being dead in the water. She was a good captain and teacher, explaining each step as she unfurled the sail. With knowledge and understanding of the process came comfort. By the time we were under way, I was enjoying the peacefulness of hearing nothing but the wind whistling through the rigging. The salt air that filled my lungs had never tasted so sweet, and riding amongst the waves had never been so soothing to my soul. We were childhood friends, this place called John's Bay and me, and I couldn't have been more grateful for the reunion. Soon I had the film footage I had come for, but I neglected to inform Captain Cindy we could go home now.

So here I sat in the dead of winter being kept alive by the sights and sounds of last summer captured on video. Never being one to hoard, I decided to share some of the video with my parents. Like me, I was sure they could use a remedy for cabin fever. Plus, it was an opportunity to pay closer attention to the conversation and be certain there were no more misinterpreted "Nose's Rock" names on my part.

My parents enjoyed hearing the birds and seeing the green grass as much as I did. There were scenes of Manhattan and their trip back to Whitehead. We were having a good time forgetting about the snow and freezing temperatures—or at least I thought we were—until out of the blue Dad made a comment.

"What are you so mad about?"

My father's words caught me off guard.

"What are you talking about, Dad?"

"Every picture of you looks like you are mad at the world," he explained.

"I'm not mad at nothing." Without thinking, I'd reverted to my childhood and sounded like a kid using double negatives. My old English teacher, Mr. Murphy, would be rolling over in his grave if he heard me say such a thing. It was not what I'd meant to say, but maybe it was closer to the truth than I realized. Why the heck was Dad talking about me being mad? It made me mad just thinking about it!

"You need to smile more." Dad hit me with another blow.

"But I *am* smiling!" I argued back. Not wanting to show him my dismay, I froze the smile on my face, trying my best to keep the conversation light.

"Well, I never!" I joked as I got to my feet and pretended that I was stomping off. But the joke was on me when I peered at my reflection in the mirror from across the room. Where did my smile go? We were having a great afternoon, and I thought I was smiling all along. However, the blank, nondescript face I saw in the mirror did not reflect that at all. I forced my face into an exaggerated smile. The muscles of my cheeks ached as I saw the corners of my mouth turn slightly upwards. It brought me back to my childhood and the times I would make faces at my mother. She would warn me to be careful that my face didn't stick that way. Were her long-ago words a premonition for this stage of my life?

Well, this just takes all the fun out of Parkinson's disease, I thought to myself. It was something I'd read about earlier in the diagnosis. The

SNOW ANGELS ON THE MOON

muscles in your face don't react as they should. You become stone-faced, frozen as if wearing a mask. Had I reached that point in the progression of the disease?

I hated to admit it, but Dad was right. I did look like I was mad at the world. However, I was far from feeling angry on the inside. I am thankful to be alive and just happy to be going on with my life. I even felt giddy about what I had accomplished over the past year in uncovering the details about the rescue. But now, evidently, my reflection did not reflect that. I explained to Dad the effect Parkinson's can have on a person's face. I assured him I was happy. It became clear that he was feeling a little sorry for having spoken up when he did. Truthfully, I was glad he had. I thanked him for his honesty. That afternoon, the old lesson proved true: Like a book, you still can't judge a person by their cover.

As we continued to watch the extra video I had filmed, it included every angle of Whitehead Light Station. My parents were taken back to a happier time as they provided their own spontaneous narration. The scenes from summer offered us all hope for tomorrow. As agonizingly long as Maine winters can seem, this one, too, promised to come to an end. Someday we would be enjoying the warmer weather again, but not soon enough.

On the ride back home, my mind turned to the disease that I have been trying to ignore for the past ten years. I think everybody tries to ignore it. Parkinson's isn't sexy enough to draw much of a crowd. It is a disease in slippers and a bathrobe that is content being confined to a nursing home. Out of sight, out of mind. That is, until someone like your kid brother gets it. Someone like Michael J. Fox. That puts a face on the disease. A face everyone loves, that can't be forgotten. Only then does it seem there is hope in finding a cure.

The more I learned about the disease, the less I knew and the more it scared me. The progression of Parkinson's is different in everybody. For the most part, it doesn't come like a thief in the night, but I have seen it progress rapidly in others. If you are lucky, it takes its sweet time. Either way, it eats away at your mobility; your muscles become rigid, sometimes making movement almost impossible. It diminishes the volume of your voice, shortens your steps, and masks your smile—which seemingly robs you of your personality. Two things I found odd about the disease were that it takes away your sense of smell and that not everyone has tremors (like we all think when we hear the word *Parkinson's*).

I remember when I was a little boy, my Auntie Thereas always called me a little "wiggle worm." She would offer me a quarter if I could sit still for ten minutes. Auntie knew it was a pretty safe bet, one that she would never have to pay out, but always did. Dyskinesia brings out the little wiggle worm in me all over again. This is cute when you are five, but not so much when you are fifty-five.

Five times a day, I take medicine that with each dose offers a three-hour window of normalcy. As the medicine wears off, the symptoms return, and the roller coaster ride begins. If the dosage is not enough or if I eat too much protein, the medicine doesn't work so well. My body feels like it is wrapped in a cocoon. I can be as rigid as the Tin Man in the *Wizard of Oz* crying out for his oil can. Over-medicate and the cure can be just as bad as the disease; it can result in dyskinesia, an involuntary muscle movement. Those times, I can be as floppy and jiggly as the Scarecrow. The only thing missing is a symptom from the Cowardly Lion. But, now that I think about it, I probably relate to him, as well, being afraid of what the disease and tomorrow will hold.

For some, it is hard to watch. People become standoffish—no more hugs, fewer handshakes. Some seem content to just look away, as if I am not in the room. In their defense, it *is* difficult to watch some days. It made me wonder if I have done the same thing to other people over my lifetime. You know what they say: "You can't really understand what someone with Parkinson's is going through until you have 'shuffled' a mile in their shoes."

My only defense (other than short bouts of normalcy with medicine) is exercise and exaggeration. Parkinson's might start with the word *park*, but that's the last thing people need to do. It's best to kick it into gear and walk, run, bike, anything to keep oneself moving.

I have an in with the exaggeration piece of it. Learning the art of storytelling from my seafaring uncles, I know a thing or two about

SNOW ANGELS ON THE MOON

embellishing. Finally, there was something I was good at that would help with my struggle against this disease. Everything I need to do must be done in an exaggerated manner. When I speak, I need to speak loudly. When I step, I need to step big. And when I smile, I need to smile almost to the point of goofiness. Exaggeration to all three would be perceived as normal to others—at least that's what I've been told—and like Knowles Rocks, I hope I've heard it right. Otherwise, I will look awfully goofy doing it.

CHAPTER 26

OH ME FATHER WAS A KEEPER

After sorting through the stacks of information that had been collected about the rescue, all the pieces were starting to fit together. Present-day 2015 faded away and there I was—a fly on the wall of a tent and it was 1958...

The campfires scattered around Camden Hills State Park didn't stand much chance of lasting throughout the night. The heavy rain pelted the canvas tents as the teens from Burleigh Hill Sailing Camp crawled into their sleeping bags. Some of the older kids had just returned from the movie, *Peyton Place*. The book by the same title was banned in many cities and towns due to its steamy content. Now, as a movie filmed in Camden, it piqued the interest of many a camper, even if it was only to get inside a warm theater and away from the cold, damp evening. The younger (more impressionable) crowd had been elected to stay behind and tend to camp.

It was the third night in a row the group had spent in Camden, and it promised to be the coldest and the wettest thus far. It was hard to imagine it was the 18th of August. "Autumn must come early in Maine" had to have been in the thoughts of the campers, most of whom were from New York. Shortly before sunrise, the clouds had wrung out the last few drops of humidity and the rain finally subsided. The campers awoke to sunshine and a brisk wind on that chilly morning. A Canadian air mass had infiltrated the northeast and was felt as far south as Philadelphia.

Those who emerged from their tents early were greeted with two obstacles: bone-chilling cold and a difficult time finding dry firewood.

SNOW ANGELS ON THE MOON

Temperatures in Camden hit a record low of forty-three degrees. The summer of 1958 was ending abruptly with the change in weather. It was both a blessing and a curse. Dressed in layers, the campers huddled by the fire to keep warm. Hurricane Cleo, a once Category IV storm, had been threatening the East Coast all week. However, the cold temperatures were now pushing it out to sea.

The five sailboats and one powerboat would soon be on their next-to-last leg of a week-long excursion along Midcoast Maine. They were scheduled to leave Camden later that day. Next stop: Tenants Harbor for the night, and the next day they would finish where they had started, in Boothbay.

The wind increased as the morning progressed. This prompted a few of the more experienced boat captains to petition camp director Lester Rhoads to remain in Camden for one more night. Clearly, it was not going to be a good day on the ocean. Unable to convince Lester, they were disappointed. He reasoned that many parents would soon be arriving in Boothbay to pick up their kids at the end of camp. The campers had been away from home for eight weeks and would be anxious to get back to their families and the "real" world.

Once the campsite was cleaned, everyone gathered around the bus listening to Lester read off the campers' names and their assigned boats. He was always careful to break up cliques and couples. It was important for the campers to have their minds totally on sailing. More than once, he was overheard stating, "There are no couples in this camp."

The crew for the blue-hulled sailboat *Debby* was set: Jeff Stark, Susan Cheever, Leslie Lewis, and Dan Granoff, all from the New York City area. The captain was camp counselor Peter Laylin from the Midwest. Peter had endured a tough year of sailing, having gone aground several times and once even losing a jib.

When it was finally time to leave, everyone loaded aboard the bus and headed for Camden Harbor. Just as they had been trained, each camper grabbed a life preserver on the way to their respective boats. As the pile dwindled, the condition of each life jacket became more ragged and worn-out. The jackets at the bottom would meet the

186

OH ME FATHER WAS A KEEPER

one-life-jacket-per-person regulations, but the chance of their keeping anyone afloat was questionable. Some crewmembers remember having five life jackets; others remember only three aboard the *Debby*.

As they prepared to leave the dock, an argument involving Lester and one of the staff flared up. The skirmish resulted in some of the boat equipment being strewn around. One of the *Debby's* bailing cans disappeared, leaving them with only one small can and a sponge.

Being first out of the harbor, the *Debby* tacked back and forth, waiting for the other boats to catch up. Then a problem occurred with their rigging. They dropped the mainsail to signal for help while the other boats sailed on by. By the time the powerboat stopped to assist, the problem was fixed, so they waved him off. The *Debby* was now a good fifteen minutes behind the others. As the lone sailboat made its way out to Penobscot Bay, it was evident that they were in for a cold, wet day of sailing.

The Coast Guard crew at Whitehead Light Station was having a busy day working on the station's twenty-foot utility boat and doing the necessary chores on the back side of the island.

That afternoon, nobody noticed the four sailboats and one powerboat making their way out through Mussel Ridge Channel.

Once they reached the open ocean, the boats turned the corner toward Tenants Harbor. Still lagging way behind, the *Debby* rounded Owls Head Light. They were getting a taste of what the ocean had to offer. The *Debby* was taking on water with each wave that crashed over the bow. Somewhere along the way, that crucial piece of equipment—the lone bailing can—was lost overboard. All they had to bail with was a sponge and their bare hands. By now, the other boats were far out of sight. Tucking back into the leeward side of the islands, the *Debby* followed the channel toward Whitehead Island. The kids started singing sea chanteys to keep up their courage.

Oh me father was a keeper of the Eddystone Light

and he slept with a mermaid one fine night.

187

From this union there came three—

A porpoise and a porgy and the other was me!

Yo, ho, ho,

The wind blows free.

Oh, for the life on the rolling sea

Back on Whitehead Island, it was time for a little relaxation before supper and the evening chores. Alan Calta, one of the other light-keepers, was trying to beat my father at horseshoes. My sister, Becky, was sleeping nearby in her playpen. My mother was down along the shore picking berries. Out of the corner of her eye, she saw a sailboat heading for open ocean. No place she would want to be on a day like this, but they appeared to be doing okay, so she went back to picking her berries.

Out on the *Debby*, the crew was standing in water almost to their knees. The weather continued to worsen. The newspaper would later report waves were as high as fifteen feet with winds increasing to forty miles per hour in Penobscot Bay. As the tiny vessel porpoised its way out of the protection of Mussel Ridge Channel, it was like an animal being led to slaughter.

The vessel became hard to control. Soon the tiller was useless. With one final wave over the bow, the *Debby* groaned its last gasp and was swamped. Susan, Leslie, and Dan were thrown into the water, while Jeffrey and Peter clung to the bow. Floorboards rose up and floated away over the gunwales. What life jackets they had flew away in the wind. Dan grabbed one as it went by and put it on. He swam the one hundred feet to retrieve another one. Just as he got there, the extra clothing he had worn to keep warm from the early morning chill started to pull him under. Panicking, Dan kicked off his pants and extra clothing and popped up to the surface. As he gasped for air, he could do nothing but watch as his clothing and high school letter jacket floated away. He grabbed the extra life preserver, swam back and put it on Leslie. None of the other three had life jackets to help keep them afloat. They could only rely on clinging to the *Debby*. If she went to the bottom, they would surely soon follow.

Back on shore, my mother was still picking berries. With her bowl mostly full, she looked up, checking on the little blue sailboat she had noticed a half hour before. She scanned the horizon and saw it off in the distance. It was barely visible, as it blended in with the bright blue ocean and the white chop, like icing on top of the waves. But something didn't look right. She ran up to the house, grabbed the binoculars, and focused in on the speck this side of the horizon. The vessel appeared to be half submerged and the mast was gone. Her heart started to pound as she ran to my father, yelling, "Russell, there's a sailboat in trouble! I think there are people in the water!"

Dad started running and barking out orders to Alan. "Call Rockland and Burnt Island! Get rescue boats coming!"

Knowing time was of the essence, Dad sprinted the quarter mile to the back side of the island where the boat was kept. He knew they were fortunate, because if it had been two weeks earlier, he would have had no boat to run to. All they would have been able to do was notify Rockland and watch helplessly as the ocean had its way. But that was then, and this was now. Dad knew his boat was too small for the task at hand and was no match for the weather. But he had no choice. He couldn't stand by and wait for the larger rescue boat to arrive; he had to attempt a rescue.

Running as fast as he could, he wished that he had a larger boat. When he got to the other side of the island, to his astonishment, there alongside the dock was a bigger boat, a lobster boat with the name *Mabel* painted on the stern. Hoping the owner was somewhere nearby, he searched the shoreline. There, on the other side of the cove, he saw a young man just stepping out of the tree line and onto the shore. Calling out loudly and waving his arms, my father tried to get his attention.

Sixteen-year-old David Gamage wasn't supposed to be on the island that day. He had been spending his summer with his grandparents on the mainland. Like all the other fishermen along the coast of

SNOW ANGELS ON THE MOON

Maine that day, he couldn't go lobstering because the seas were too rough. Out of the blue and for no apparent purpose, David's grandfather needed to go out to Whitehead. Maybe it was to check on their cottage, maybe not, David wasn't sure. All he knew was that visiting the island had become rarer and rarer since his grandfather had retired from being the lightkeeper on Whitehead. Now, as he tinkered away in his workshop, without saying a word, David slipped out the door and made his way past the cottage and onto the shore. Hearing screams, he looked up to see someone on the light station dock jumping up and down, waving his arms like a madman. David raced to the dock—where he met my father for the first time. Dad explained the situation and asked to commandeer the boat. Instinctively, David jumped aboard, and my father followed. David pushed the start button and the engine roared to life while Dad cast off the lines. Soon they were speeding out of the cove.

By now, the exhausted crew from the *Debby* had been in the water for almost an hour. The mind-numbing cold of the Atlantic was draining the life from their bodies. All eyes were on Leslie. She was shaking, turning blue, and faintly weeping. It looked as though at any moment she would let go of the boat and fade away into the deep.

CHAPTER 27

AN OPEN PALM

What a difference a day makes. It was only yesterday the campers from Burleigh Hill had set sail from Vinalhaven bound for Camden Harbor. It was a picture-perfect afternoon along the coast of Maine. The calm before the storm. Taking her turn at the tiller, Susan was in charge. As the sail caught the full force of the wind, she could feel the boat lift out of the water as if to puff out its chest bragging, "Look at me! Look at me!" Susan was on top of the world. Finally, after eight weeks of sailing camp, she really felt like a sailor! It was what her father had wanted, and by golly, she had done it. Now she couldn't wait to get home and take her father sailing to show off her fancy new skills.

As euphoric as yesterday had been, this afternoon was the complete opposite. Susan wasn't sure if she would ever see her father again. Like Dr. Jekyll and Mr. Hyde, the Atlantic had changed overnight from a playground into a battleground. Waves exploded like mortar shells around Susan and the four other campers as they clung to the *Debby*. They had no idea that hurricane Cleo was passing by far out to sea but was still close enough to send gusting winds and mounting waves in their direction.

If it was any consolation (and it wasn't), Susan knew she would not be the first to die. Sadly, that distinction would soon go to her friend Leslie. Susan wasn't sure what to do next. Maybe she could make it to an island that she saw off in the distance. It would appear every so often when the waves lifted her up to a higher vantage point. She was a pretty good swimmer, but the little island was too far and the sea too rough, and she was too tired and too cold. She decided to stay with her friends, hang onto the boat, and wait. Wait for what? She didn't

SNOW ANGELS ON THE MOON

like the answer that came to mind. If only this was a dream or one of her father's short stories. After all, he was John Cheever, the author. With a few strokes of the pen, he could rewrite the ending with a much happier outcome. But tragically, for Susan, this was all too real, and she knew there would be no heroes today.

Dan was in the water next to her. Without talking to Susan, he was contemplating the same thought: Could he make it to the island? Maybe he could and bring back help. It was better than staying here and waiting for nothing. Looking up, he saw the crashing waves against the rocky shore, an obstacle no one could survive, and thought better of the idea.

Jeff didn't think he was going to die that day. Hypothermia has a way of clouding people's minds. Just because you believe it doesn't necessarily make it so. He had never been so cold in his life. In an attempt to escape the frigid ocean, Jeff would climb onto the bow, which was sticking out of the water. He would then shimmy up the mast as best he could, only to find that his weight would roll the *Debby* to one side, and both he and the mast would dip back into the water. It seemed like he was stuck in a never-ending cycle to try to get warm.

Having left the protection of the back side of the island, the lobster boat *Mabel* encountered a wall of defiance. Battling the wind and waves, suddenly the engine sputtered to a stop. There at the mercy of the ocean, Dad and David looked at each other wide-eyed. What happened? Are we out of gas? The motor's silence was deafening.

With the wind quick to push them sideways, water splashed over the starboard railing. Keeping his head about him, David checked the controls and discovered a hammer had fallen off the dashboard, hit the throttle, and killed the engine. He started it once again and soon they were back under way.

Peter had lost all sense of time as to how long they were in the water. Panic had not yet set in, although he had a feeling of overwhelming regret that he would never see his mother or father again. Then, out of nowhere, an angel appeared. Peter looked up and couldn't believe his eyes. A speeding boat was coming in their direction with water spraying outward from its bow, giving the appearance of angel wings. They all started yelling and screaming for help. Was this possible? Were they really being rescued? In the next moment, the lobster boat changed course and turned away from the sailboat *Debby*. Don't they see us? Their hearts fell into despair as the boat went further and further away.

On the lobster boat *Mabel*, my father ran up next to David and started firing questions. "Hey, what are you doing? Where are you going?" David pointed down at the ledges barely hidden underneath the water. Dad nodded that he understood and knew at that moment there could be no better man at the helm that day. As a lobsterman, David knew the surrounding waters. Better still, he knew the ledges. As this was his grandfather's boat, he was more than familiar with the *Mabel* and knew its capabilities. If Dad had commandeered the boat and attempted to go it alone, the results could have been disastrous.

Maneuvering around the ledges, David aimed the *Mabel* back in the direction of the sailboat. Seeing the angel wings almost upon them, the exhausted crew realized they were saved and became silent, thanking God for His kindness.

The *Mabel* came up alongside the mostly submerged sailboat. As the two boats converged, the force of the waves could have easily crushed whatever or whoever found its way in between the two. Dad plunged his arms into the water and wrapped them around the first body they came to. Bending far down over the side of the boat, he could feel himself losing his balance. He locked his legs against the railing to keep from being pulled overboard. The last thing any of them needed was another person in the water to rescue.

Using all the strength Dad could muster was not enough to pull the first water-soaked, exhausted teenager aboard. Dad's body had contorted itself into such an awkward position that all he could do was hang over the side, off balance. He held on for what seemed like an eternity. He couldn't pull them aboard and he darn sure was not about to let them go.

SNOW ANGELS ON THE MOON

Suddenly, a hand reached down in front of Dad and grabbed the teen by the scruff of the neck. It was David, who had run back to help. Their combined strength was just enough to pull the first survivor out of the water and into the boat. They repeated the action four more times. One by one, the doomed crew was pulled up and out of the unforgiving ocean. Once everyone was on board, they huddled around the engine's muffler to keep warm.

As Dad tied the rope around *Debby's* bow, one of the boys asked to go back aboard the half-sunken sailboat. He wanted to retrieve his shoes, which had his wallet neatly tucked inside. The rescuers wouldn't entertain such nonsense. David put the boat in gear and tried towing the *Debby*. Being mostly under water, the strain was too much, and the tow rope snapped.

Leslie appeared to be incoherent and had stopped shaking. In concern for her, they abandoned the *Debby* and raced to the back side of the island. They were met on the dock with blankets and taken back to the lighthouse. My mother took Susan and Leslie to her bedroom. Opening her bureau drawer, she said, "Take what you need." Leslie disappeared into the bathroom, where she became violently ill. My mother rendered what aid she could.

Dad and David returned to the stormy sea to rescue the sailboat. They could not leave it out there abandoned because it would be a hazard to navigation for others.

The kids were safe in the lighthouse, wrapped in blankets and drinking hot tea. Watching from the window, they saw a powerboat approaching from Tenants Harbor. It weaved from side to side as if looking for something in the waves. Then it stopped and pulled something out of the water and took off to the back side of the island. It was the camp powerboat from Burleigh Hill. They had found a floorboard from the *Debby*. Thinking the worst, they were racing to report the missing sailboat and the loss of its crew to the Coast Guard. When the powerboat reached the back side of the island, they found the *Debby* tied to a mooring and heard the news that the campers were safe inside the lighthouse.

By the time the commander from Rockland arrived in a rescue boat,

David Gamage had done his good deed for the day and was just leaving the dock. One of the Coast Guard crew ran up to him inquiring, "Are you one of the victims?"

"Nope, I'm not one of the victims. The victims are up at the lighthouse," David replied. With that, the commander and his entourage disappeared into the woods. David went back to his grandfather, who was none the wiser about the afternoon's events. When questioned about all the commotion over on the Coast Guard dock, David told his grandfather it had something to do with towing in a sailboat. He saw no need to offer any more than that.

Later in the evening, Dad fired up the station's utility boat and took the crew of the *Debby* to Spruce Head. There they met the camp bus that would take them back to Boothbay. The excitement for the day was over, but Dad and Alan still had those evening chores to do.

———————————

The next day was like any other day. Mother found herself making a pie with those berries. Dad was busy with his chores. It was as if the rescue had never happened. But the chest that held the winter blankets was now empty, and there were fewer clothes in my mother's bureau drawer. Hopefully, they could save enough money to replace those blankets before the snow flies, and my mother said she had enough clothes anyway. By now, the kids were back at camp or at home—wherever that was. At the base in Rockland, a petty officer was typing up a letter of commendation that never quite made its way into my father's file. There were no medals, no fanfare. Why would there be? He was just doing his job, tending light off the coast of Maine.

CHAPTER 28

A TINGE OF RED

With the rescue story safely compiled and written into a script, it was time to see if I could create this movie that kept playing over and over inside my head. Although not a filmmaker, I did have some experience in taking a few home movies over the years. We bought our first video camera in the late '80s when the kids were small. It was a luxury that seemed more like a necessity. Either way, it was one we couldn't afford, if not for all the Christmas wreaths.

Looking back, it was a fun way to make some extra money (although Heidi and my mother might remember it differently). We would put the kids on the toboggan and trudge our way across the frozen tundra of my Uncle Ed's snow-covered field. Reaching the edge of the woods, we would fill canvas bags with balsam boughs and stack them on the sled. The longer the wreath season progressed, the deeper into the forest we would need to delve. When we couldn't fit another fir tip into the bags and another bag on the toboggan, we would put the kids on top to help secure the cargo. They would hold on for dear life as we made our way back home.

The kitchen table was hijacked for the duration as it became the workshop for the wreath-making Santas. The house smelled wonderful, but it looked like a Christmas tree had exploded inside. Gene Autry was singing "Rudolph, the Red-Nosed Reindeer" on the stereo. The volume was down to a whisper, more for ambience than for entertainment. Taking turns at the table, my mother and Heidi would clutch clumps of boughs and wind them onto metal hoops. Their fingers quickly became cracked and sore. Every so often, a groan would rise from their lips as one of them poked herself with the end of the wire. Ouch! I must admit, the red and green on their fingertips looked pain-

SNOW ANGELS ON THE MOON

fully festive. Add a pretty red bow to the wreathes, like a cherry on top of an ice cream sundae, and the creation was complete.

Every dollar that came in was stashed away in a cookie jar on the counter. With the last wreath sold, the jar's contents were emptied out and traded for a video camera. As with any new toy, I couldn't put it down. This resulted in hours of video of school concerts and kids' ballgames that I am sure no one will ever take the time to watch. But every so often, a minute's worth of video made all the hard work worthwhile as we captured a precious moment in time, a glimpse of our babies' race to adulthood or the belly laugh of a loved one now long gone.

Back then, my video technique was more about movie-taking than moviemaking. It was point-and-shoot, capture the moment. Making this film was different. It needed to meld music, narration, photographs, and video to tell a story. I had already learned a lot about the software and the process in the first few go-rounds of making *Looking for a Hero*. Should I fade to black or fade to white? Pan up or pan down? I soon learned every movement has a meaning. Even the length of a pause could add or take away from the story.

With every new rendition of *Hero,* the length had doubled, one minute to two minutes, then two minutes to five. The movie had already ballooned to a whopping ten minutes since its conception. (That can be an eternity while watching slides from your next-door neighbor's trip to Altoona.) Someone warned me I might be in danger of losing my audience if I dared make it any longer. All I knew was that I just needed to tell the story and let the chips, along with the minutes and seconds, fall where they may.

With hours of video to choose from, it was obvious that most of the material would end up on the cutting room floor. Thus, my discovery of the dilemma directors like Steven Spielberg and Ron Howard must face every day. What part of your life's creative work needs to be sacrificed to tell the story? That's funny. Here I am making something comparable to a high school slide-show presentation and suddenly I'm Steven Spielberg? Yet something down deep told me those two filmmakers would have to agree. When the lights go dim in the theater, *they* need to disappear into the darkness along with everybody and everything else. From that point on, it's all about the story.

So began the long process of making and editing the movie in post-production. At one point during the winter, the task became grueling. I had seen way too much of the same video and spoken too much of the same narrative while trying to produce that perfect clip. I couldn't let my stuttering interfere with the integrity of the film. Each word had been painstakingly chosen, not for fluency, but to reflect the facts concerning the rescue as I continued to make more fodder for the cutting room floor.

Finally, one day in February, the voiceover was complete. I exhaled a sigh of relief. The pain was over. I looked down at my hands and saw the familiar slight tinge of red on my fingers. It was dried blood, remnants from my childhood bag of tricks used to stifle a stutter. As a boy, whenever I anticipated getting hung up on a word, I'd dig my fingernails into the skin of my opposite hand. At some point the pain would override the struggle and the words flowed flawlessly. I'd used the method more times than I'd care to admit. Trading pain for fluency is nothing I would recommend, but at twelve years old, it was a small price to pay to fit in with the other kids. And now, somehow, after all these years, I was doing it again. One more item to add to my list of things that resurfaced while uncovering the details about the rescue. If there is one thing this journey has taught me, it's that you can't revisit the past without awakening some emotions—and possibly some pain—along with it.

With the movie now complete, it was easy to see that most of the details had been provided by the crew of the *Debby* and David Gamage. Dad's memories seemed to have faded over the years. He no longer remembers pulling the campers out of the water. He must have been running on pure adrenaline. But clearly, the memory of losing his best friend played an important role that day. It made him all the more determined not to have these five teens meet the same fate. Not on his watch!

Once the full story unfolded in front of me, I realized what a house of cards the rescue had been built on. One small miscue or a few delicate seconds in either direction and the news headline would have read differently that next day. The ocean would have been satisfied, licking its chops as the paper read "Five Campers Drown off the Coast of Maine." Five families would have been mourning that week, maybe six. Dad admits he didn't have much confidence in the station's utility boat as he sprinted down the path at Whitehead Island that day.

In hoping for a critique on the film, I began to invite some close friends to my home to view the movie with instructions to be brutally honest. Well, maybe not brutal, but honest. With their encouragement, I entered the movie in three film festivals, all in Maine. Three is always a good number. Third time's a charm or three strikes you're out; we would see. Soon I discovered the problem with film festivals: the waiting. It was late February and the first one did not promise to get back to me until June.

Meanwhile, I was contacted by David Gamage. He had been doing some investigation of his own with the hope of getting Dad some form of recognition. He discovered, unbeknownst to us, that the Coast Guard had conducted a second investigation. They found a note within Dad's record indicating that he should have received a commendation back in 1959, when David received his. However, they never did find a copy of the official letter that should have been included in Dad's file. Somehow all that didn't seem very important anymore.

Not wanting to sit on my hands waiting for responses from the film festivals, I started showing the film at nursing homes and community groups from Kittery to Camden. It was a treat to be able to show off my parents, who faithfully tagged along.

As spring turned to summer, the rejection letters arrived.

The Maine Film Festival. "Thanks, but no thanks." Strike one.

The Camden Film Festival. "Although we appreciate your submission..." Strike two.

With only a few weeks left in the summer, I had one more time at bat, the International Maritime Film Festival (IMFF). In late August when the e-mail arrived in my in-box, I wasn't in a hurry to open it. The longer I could put it off, the longer I could go without feeling rejected

A TINGE OF RED

again. Finally finding the courage to click on the e-mail, I was soon on the phone to my parents. "Hi, Mom. Just wanted to tell you to keep the first weekend in October open because we're going to a film festival."

CHAPTER 29

FINALLY, A FILM FESTIVAL

Now that I'm older, summer doesn't depart with any sadness, not when I have September waiting in the wings. The neighborhood kids all head back to school as the summer visitors from away, go away. But I must admit I kind of miss them both when they are not around.

Autumn brings a different atmosphere to Maine, a slower pace. It tends to be a laid-back, older crowd, more of what we're used to. Summer may have its one night of fireworks on July 4th, but fall has its own colorful display lasting for weeks. The leaves enjoy one last fling as the maples and oaks explode with bright reds and yellows among a contrasting sea of steadfast evergreens. This truly is my favorite time of year.

It was the last Monday in September and it promised to be a good week. My family was looking forward to attending the International Maritime Film Festival. The name alone sounded impressive. It was still hard for me to believe they were going to show my movie on the big screen. That being said, it would not be the highlight of the weekend. The film would need to take a backseat to the reunion of my parents and one of the rescued "kids," Jeff Stark. But before any of that could happen, I had to get through my regular workweek.

For a Monday, it was an odd one, a rarity. Heidi and I never take Mondays off unless, of course, there's a funeral or a doctor's appointment. Thankfully, that wasn't the case this morning. However, a few weeks before, Dan Granoff had showed my video to some friends of his from Georgia. They had been planning a trip to Maine and wanted to meet with Heidi and me. I must admit it was a puzzlement why someone would want to take time away from their vacation to meet us. Nonetheless, we had set aside the last Monday in September for

SNOW ANGELS ON THE MOON

the visit. That was the day Dan's friends were to travel between Bar Harbor and Portland. We were to meet up at the Botanical Gardens in Boothbay for lunch.

Wanting to be sure there were no problems at work for the day, I stopped in for an hour or so. I walked around the shop floor as part of my usual morning routine, checking on the automated machines I had helped build over the years and checking in with people. Back in my office, I logged onto the computer, where I could monitor and control many of the plant systems. Bringing up the surveillance cameras, in a few short minutes I had gathered the details of the comings and goings that had happened in the plant throughout the evening. I even saw myself getting out of my truck and walking into work, something I witnessed every morning.

Hearing footsteps coming up the stairs, heavy, deliberate, and unmistakable, I knew they belonged to my business partner, Chad Hanna. After working with him for nearly two decades, I had learned he had one speed. Every step he took up the stairs or in his life was the same. It was well thought out, not just for his own benefit, but for those around him. Chad had become like the brother I'd never had. I still remember the day I approached him about starting our own business. Having already been diagnosed with Parkinson's, I was a year into the disease. I reminded him about the unknowns of my illness and said I would understand if he thought the business venture would be too much of a risk. But to my surprise, he told me that none of us knows what tomorrow holds, and the partnership was formed.

As Chad came into our shared office, he appeared zombielike.

"Oh, no; what's the matter this time?" I asked, leaning back in my chair and folding my hands behind my head.

He sat down across the room, not offering to look in my direction.

"I just spoke to the owners, and they hit me with a bombshell." I could tell Chad didn't want to say the next words that came out of his mouth. He said it like ripping off a Band-Aid. (I guess there is no better way to hear it.) "They say they don't need your services anymore, Russ. They want me to stay on, but I am not going to. I'm leaving also." The pain in Chad's voice was hard to bear.

FINALLY, A FILM FESTIVAL

To say that the news was unexpected would be an understatement, although looking back now, maybe it wasn't so unexpected after all. I wasn't blind. I saw the progression of my disease as it played out on the surveillance cameras every morning.

Chad and I had both worked for the company for nearly a decade before starting our partnership. We had branched out, taking on projects for other companies; however, the bulk of our work was still back at the manufacturing plant where we began. Now, with their decision to keep only one of us, we both knew our other accounts wouldn't pay the bills. It certainly was a death blow to our business.

"We can't have both of us looking for a job at the same time. You'd better stay on," I advised. My words were more of a reaction than a thoughtful response. But it seemed logical.

Chad went on to explain their decision, but honestly, it didn't really matter at that point. I had been around long enough to understand the rigors of business and that some days it's a necessity to make the difficult decisions for the good of the company. I could accept that. However, the hardest thing to accept was not being given the courtesy of being told directly. It was akin to being kicked to the curb but felt more like a kick in the pants. All I knew was that I had walked through those shop doors and worked in some capacity for close to nineteen years, and now, in the blink of an eye, that was about to change.

As I looked at the clock, I suddenly remembered Wayne and Trudy, the mystery couple from Georgia. Still a little stunned, I walked out to my truck unaware of any of my surroundings. Needing to first pick up Heidi, I was not sure how I would tell her the news, but somehow I did. Probably, like Chad did with me, quick like a Band-Aid. Heidi's reaction skipped right over disbelief and shock (the first stage of grief) and went straight to anger.

Our ride to Boothbay was done in silence, but not one you could ever categorize as peaceful. The whole morning's events had to be put aside as my mind needed a diversion, and meeting Trudy and Wayne in the Coastal Maine Botanical Gardens proved to be just the ticket. We talked about how I'd made the movie. They wanted to know the story behind the story. Their words were kind and uplifting, just what

SNOW ANGELS ON THE MOON

I needed to hear right then. Walking around the gardens, the aroma of the many flowers combined to override the loss of my sense of smell, a condition of Parkinson's. The beauty and the serenity were in sharp contrast to a typical noisy, hectic Monday on the manufacturing shop floor. The morning's troubles were gone, at least for the moment. Reality would soon be back knocking on my door. But for now, this meeting, this appointment that had been planned on my calendar for weeks, was just the salve my soul needed.

The next morning, I went to work to pack up my stuff and leave for the last time. Chad helped me carry out my belongings. He had come to his senses and agreed that he would stay on. (However, in less than two weeks Chad would reconsider that decision and leave also.)

That week certainly started off on the downside. It seemed I went through the process of grieving tenfold, not with just losing my work but with losing the daily contact with people that had meant so much to me. I had withstood worse than this in my lifetime, but the Parkinson's challenge did seem to limit my opportunities. After ten years of battling the disease, I hadn't let it stop me yet, and I wasn't about to let it do so now.

In preparation for the film festival, we made reservations at a Bucksport hotel for two nights for the upcoming weekend (quite an expense when you don't have a job). I talked myself in and out of canceling the hotel several times over the course of the week. Finally, reasoning that it would give Dad a place to go if he grew tired during the festival, we made the decision to go on as planned.

Friday came and we were ready for our trip to Bucksport. It had been a town full of mystery and intrigue for me growing up. When I was ten years old, Dad was having a lobster boat made on Beal's Island, down off Jonesport. It seemed like every weekend we piled into the car for the six-hour round trip. Upon arrival we would get out just long enough to stretch our legs and see the one plank they had fit into place since our last visit. Building a wooden boat was a slow and painstaking process, and if you consider the ride down and back every week to check on the progress, I would add pain*ful*.

We were always in too much of a hurry to stop anywhere fun, except for an occasional visit to Perry's Nut House in Belfast. Dad would pick up cashews for the ride, and, if we were good, Becky and I could buy something, too. We'd usually choose fake doggy doo-doo or real live Mexican jumping beans. You can never have too much of that stuff lying around. As we continued on to Beal's Island, my mother would ration out cashews to the backseat, reminding us that they were meant to be eaten one at a time and not in handfuls. Oh, no; what happened to the Mexican jumping bean? Did I eat it by accident? Too scared to tell my parents, I remained silent for the rest of the trip. I felt a flip-flop in my belly for days.

Continuing up the coast, we'd pass through Bucksport, which felt as if we were bypassing Disneyland. As a kid I wasn't above begging, and I am sure I made the fact known that we needed to stop there. Then one day it happened! Dad pulled into the parking lot of Fort Knox. I felt like a soldier as I stood next to the cannons pretending to fire over the river. *Boom!* I crawled over every inch of the place, exploring all the nooks and crannies and secret passageways, never finding any of the gold that was supposed to be kept there. Later, Dad explained there were two Fort Knoxes—one with gold and one without. It figures the one in Maine would be the one without.

We crossed "Suspense Bridge" leading to Verona Island. Dad drove really slowly this time, so we could savor the view. We were so high up, it was scary but exhilarating. I later found out it was not called *Suspense Bridge,* which always sounded like a bridge that lived up to its name. It actually was a *suspension* bridge.

After crossing the next smaller bridge, to my delight, instead of turning right to follow Route 1, we turned left and drove through downtown Bucksport. What a treat! The stores and sidewalks were full of people. Reaching the other end of town, we stopped and watched the big logging trucks and the busyness of the mill. We could park right across the road and have a front-row seat. My eyes went everywhere. Then, going back through town, we made one more stop: We pulled over at the cemetery so I could get a good look at that haunted gravestone.

Up until that day, I had only seen quick glimpses of it as we sped by on our previous trips to Beal's Island. The name "Buck" was carved in

SNOW ANGELS ON THE MOON

raised letters out of the stone, and a water stain in the form of a leg with a pointed toe told of a witch's curse. As Dad told the story, the grave belonged to the founder of Bucksport, who was also a judge. He had condemned a witch to be burned at the stake. She cursed his grave as the fire was ignited at her feet. Her dog ran up to save her, and while he pulled on her leg, it came off and rolled out of the fire. Soon after the judge died, the leg appeared on his headstone. Legend has it that his relatives had the stone replaced and still the leg returned. The story, like a rerun on TV, would be told every time we passed by the graveyard. It never seemed to fail to send shivers down the spines of kids in the backseat of a car heading to Beal's Island.

For a kid, this little town of Bucksport had it all! Coming back for the weekend as an adult, it still felt the same way. The difference between then and now was that the "Suspense Bridge" had been replaced by the Penobscot Narrows Bridge, the paper mill at the other end of town was abandoned, and there were too many empty parking spots in the not-so-busy streets. In the way of Millinocket and other mill towns, many in Bucksport had lost their livelihood. On this visit, I could relate more to their situation than ever before.

We checked into the hotel and had just enough time to freshen up before walking to the Alamo Theater. Heidi and I slipped into the crowd at the festival's Meet and Greet. Mingling has never been my forte, so we stood over in a corner, standing on the sidelines as though watching a sporting event. I was surprised to see so many people chatting away as they stood at bar tables that were scattered around the lobby. Did they all know each other? It sure seemed that way.

As I scanned the room, to my delight, I saw my "friend with no name" (from my weekend retreat on Whitehead Light Station) walking in. Chuckling to myself, I knew she had a name that I could never forget now. She had once offered me a comforting smile and a pat on my shoulder when I needed it most. We crossed the room and welcomed Pat with a hug. She had brought a gentleman friend along, and after introductions, we visited until it was time to go in to see the first film. (Oh, no; what was her friend's name again?! I guess some things never change.)

FINALLY, A FILM FESTIVAL

The festival organizers had only scheduled the showing of one movie that evening. It was an interesting story about plastics in the ocean breaking down and finding their way into pockets where they congregate and become a hazard to the sea life. As documentaries go, the filmmaker had done his job in creating sympathy for the plight of the sea creatures. He was also on hand and had a wonderful Q&A session afterwards. It impressed upon me that I had a lot to learn about being a filmmaker and that this weekend was probably just the beginning.

By noontime on Saturday, faces in the crowd became familiar. Of course, it helped that some of my friends had battled the leaf-peeper traffic up Route 1 to offer their support. The movies were interesting and tugged at everyone's emotions. After seeing so many polished and well-made films, I feared mine would pale in comparison.

In between films as I mingled, I couldn't help but overhear conversations in the lobby. One caught my interest above the rest. A gentleman had been talking to the movie projectionist, asking for any inside info on the ones he liked best. The projectionist told him that, of all the films, two were must-sees. They had everything a movie should have. One of them was *Looking for a Hero*. Oh my, did I just hear that right? The projectionist! What better endorsement could there be? Who cares what Siskel and Ebert or members of the Academy think? Give me input from someone who lives and breathes movies and by this stage of life has seen it all. I am waiting for the day when a director steps to the mic while accepting his Oscar and says what is really on his mind: "I would like to thank the Academy for this great honor. But what I really would like to know is *what does the projectionist think?*" If I had come to the festival looking for kudos, there they were. I could go home now. But it wasn't about that.

If there was one thing I had learned through this journey, it was not about bringing people together to tell a story that mattered most; it was about telling a story that brings people together. If I could do that by sharing my film and reuniting my parents with Jeff Stark at the same time, then I could truly count the weekend a success.

As the crowd waited in the lobby for the start of the movie scheduled before mine, I knew we were cutting it close. Jeff was to have flown

SNOW ANGELS ON THE MOON

out from New York City earlier in the morning and arrive in Bangor by noon. He needed to rent a car and then find his way to Bucksport. It was all doable—that is, if everything happened on time and according to plan. The lobby cleared out as everyone migrated back into the theater for the next movie, and still there was no Jeff. I had my concerns.

CHAPTER 30

GETTING MY BEARINGS

As I sat through the first few minutes of the film showing before mine, I didn't have a clue what it was about. However, that was not a reflection on the filmmaker or his finished product. I am sure it was a fine piece of work. I was the problem. My thoughts were with Jeff Stark somewhere between Manhattan and the main entrance to the Alamo Theater.

Suddenly, motion on the very edge of my peripheral vision grabbed my attention. Two silhouettes slowly descended the aisle. My eyes followed their progress as they stopped and started several times in their search for seats, finally settling in the front row. With my hopes replenished, I breathed a sigh of relief; it had to be Jeff, didn't it?

When the house lights came up at the end of the film my suspicions were confirmed. There was Jeff standing in the front row, scanning the theater. I waved but didn't catch his eye. Any direct route was blocked by people, so I detoured to the back of the theater where my parents were seated. It was not my best idea. Now I faced the audience flocking to the lobby as though battling summer traffic in Wiscasset for a lobster roll at Red's Eats. Standing there, I couldn't wait any longer. Damn the torpedoes, I thought as I began making my way upstream.

Since mine was the only face pointing in his direction, Jeff spotted me almost immediately. Reaching out for a welcoming handshake, seeing Jeff again was like greeting an old friend. He turned to his traveling companion and introduced her as his roommate, Julie. Escorting them back up the aisle, I reciprocated by introducing each of my friends and family members, saving my father for last.

Little did the audience know the story they were about to watch on the screen was continuing to play itself out in the back of the theater.

211

SNOW ANGELS ON THE MOON

What appeared to some like two old friends blocking the aisle in conversation was actually a reunion almost six decades in the making. When these two had first met in the open Atlantic, there had been no time for formalities. Now, years later, Dad offered his hand once again. This time, instead of hanging over the side of a boat, he was seated in a wheelchair. The hand that reached back belonged to Jeff Stark, a successful attorney from Manhattan who had served as a New York Supreme Court judge. But all I saw was a strapping young lightkeeper shaking hands with a water-soaked, exhausted teenage boy from a summer camp. Witnessing the reunion was a dream come true, and I couldn't wait to be included in their conversation over our dinner planned for later that evening.

The preparations over the last year and a half were finally complete. Everything was in place: the heroic story on film, the giant movie screen, and a captive audience. I pushed my father's wheelchair into the back row. It was the perfect location. From that vantage point, he could see the story unfold before him once again, but better yet, he would see the audience's reaction. I made my way down the aisle hoping to locate myself somewhere in the middle of the audience, where I could feel its heartbeat. However, the only seat where I wouldn't disturb anyone had me banished to the front row.

I slouched low in the seat, not to get comfortable, but to make myself less of an obstacle to those behind me. As the lights went down, the screen came to life with the cackling of seagulls playfully bickering over breakfast. The sounds of the shore gave way to gentle strokes on piano keys, and eventually my own unfamiliar voice as the narrator filled the room. The tone was set. As the audience chuckled on cue, everyone and everything in the theater faded into the shadows.

With the rolling of the final credits, the story was told. Music continued to play in the background, but the silence was deafening. I wasn't sure if the quietness of the audience was a good thing or not. I should have taken note of their reaction at the end of the other films. Were they waiting for the words *The End* to appear out of courtesy before they could applaud? If so, it might be a long wait, because it wasn't happening. Just before the dedication was supposed to appear on the screen,

212

GETTING MY BEARINGS

the room went black. We sat in silence and darkness that seemed to go on forever. There was no talking. I didn't even hear people breathing. It was a feeling of abandonment. Could this be how the campers had felt clinging to a sinking sailboat on the edge of the Atlantic, or how my father had felt weathering a terror-filled night alone in a lighthouse? Somehow the glitch in the projection room changed the punctuation at the end of the movie from a period to an exclamation point. The simple message *Don't take your life for granted* was driven home.

Finally, like a sunrise, the lights performed their heroics as they slowly came up and chased away the darkness. Polite applause began as a trickle at one end of the theater and cascaded its way across to the other side. I wasn't sure if people were clapping for the movie or the fact that the lights had come back on.

Aaron, one of the festival's organizers, made his way to the stage. I had given him a list of people in the film who were also in the audience and confided that I might be a little too emotional to read it myself.

As Aaron started to speak, it wasn't what I'd expected. Admitting that the film had hit a little too close to home, he confessed that he might have as much trouble introducing my family as I would. There was an emotion in his voice that seemed to be speaking for us all.

I started to walk up on stage as Aaron announced the names. I had no thoughts or anxiety about stuttering or my Parkinson's. There was no room in my being for such trivial concerns, just a feeling of pride knowing who I would share the stage with. My thoughts turned to David Gamage, who had another obligation that day. But I knew he was there in spirit.

When Aaron got to Jeff's name, he paused and asked if he had arrived from the airport yet. I nodded. He then invited everyone to the stage. First, I saw Jeff rise out of his seat and make his way to the front.

Then, looking to the back of the theater, I was horrified to see my father attempting to get out of his wheelchair. At that moment, was he a twenty-seven-year-old lightkeeper again reporting for duty? Afraid he might fall, I bolted from the stage to help Dad get back to his chair. I was grateful when the man sitting next to him rose up and coaxed him back down. By that time, Heidi had arrived on scene from three seats

213

SNOW ANGELS ON THE MOON

over, where she took control and started pushing Dad to the stage. Relieved and thankful, I walked down one side of the aisle as Dad was wheeled down the other. The symbolism wasn't lost on me as we traveled two different paths to the same end, much like our own lives.

Once we were in position, Aaron stepped down off the stage and leaned back against the railing. His relaxed posture partway between the audience and the stage was not one of a master of ceremonies. However, it was masterful because it created a collective feeling of ease.

Those of us on stage took turns answering questions. Even Dad grabbed the microphone to answer a question or two. All the time, Jeff stood next to Dad's wheelchair with his hand resting on my father's shoulder. He then stepped to the microphone to thank Dad for saving his life. My emotions were ready to burst as Jeff paused for a brief second and turned to my father, thanking him again on behalf of his son and then again for his grandchild. The response from the audience filled the theater with stillness.

As we left the stage, the audience rose in unison to its feet, not to leave for intermission but to applaud. I slowed my pace to allow Dad time to bask in the standing ovation. Pushing his wheelchair out to the lobby, I left him in a corner and faded into the woodwork. He wasn't alone for long, as people swarmed around him to shake his hand and offer him hugs. Grown men lined up one by one, kneeling to look my father in the eye and thank him for his service.

As the lobby cleared, everyone went back into the theater to watch the last block of movies for the afternoon. That is, everyone except our little group. We opted in favor of a reunion dinner and the chance to spend time with Jeff and Julie. Pushing my father's wheelchair out through the theater doors, next stop: the Angler's Restaurant in Searsport.

We were a party of eight around the table that really *felt* like a party. Our group consisted of Jeff and Julie, my parents, my sister Becky and my niece Lindsay, rounded out by Heidi and me. The conversation kept us all entertained with the downside being that time was racing by way too fast. There was nothing I could do (short of sitting in a dentist's chair) to slow down time, so I surrendered and tried to soak it all in.

GETTING MY BEARINGS

My father was in storytelling mode, which was a good thing. Unfortunately, the bad thing for my mother was that he had left his filter at home. This is not a problem when you are down on the wharf with the other fishermen, but in a restaurant, it made my mother a little panicky about which colorful story he might tell next. I must say, Dad behaved himself as best he could. He only told one story that made my mother cringe. Jeff graciously took it all in stride and was kind in his response in handling my father.

As we finished our meal, Jeff announced he had a story of his own to share. A few short weeks before, he had been cleaning out his attic and found some old books he no longer wanted. A friend of his offered to sell them and they would split the money.

Labor Day weekend was upon them when the friend stopped back in and gave Jeff his share of the earnings. Just as he was about to leave, the friend turned around and said he "almost forgot." Before he sold any books, he always thumbed through the pages in case someone had left cash or anything interesting between the pages.

Jeff reached inside his jacket and pulled out a tall thin card. Turning to me, he said, "This is what he found, and now I am giving it to you."

On the front was a picture of a wanted poster from the Old West. It was tacked to a tree complete with a cactus in the background. The poster read "Wanted Alive." Opening the card sent chills through my body. It was from Leslie Lewis. There, in her own handwriting, was an invitation to come to her house for a Burleigh Hill reunion party she'd scheduled just a few months after the rescue.

"There you go; you now have Leslie's DNA," Jeff remarked, making us all chuckle.

As the card was handed around the table, I was amazed at how it had been kept safe for so long, only to be unknowingly discarded by Jeff. Later saved by his hero, book-selling friend, who had thankfully given the card a second chance on life. It was more than just an interesting anecdote; it was a hand-delivered message through the decades from Leslie herself. Her times at Burleigh Hill must have been happy ones, as she wanted them to continue beyond the summer. The rescue had given her a second chance, and apparently, she was going to make the

215

SNOW ANGELS ON THE MOON

most of it. I had come to terms earlier with the fact that the mystery of Leslie Lewis probably would remain a mystery. The card didn't change that, but it gave me closure, and somehow, down deep, I knew Leslie was okay.

As the waitress polled the table about dessert, one by one we declined until she came to Jeff. He put the evening into perspective with one final gesture as he ordered a giant cream-puff pastry with eight spoons. We did more than share a dessert, we shared a bond and a memory that we would cherish for years to come.

Once outside the restaurant, we lingered in the parking lot, not wanting the day to end. As I thanked Jeff for helping to make the day special, he left me with an embrace and these words: "Don't ever stop telling your stories."

With that, we all loaded into separate cars and dispersed in three different directions: Jeff and Julie back to Bangor to catch an early-morning flight, my parents back to Bristol because nothing feels better than sleeping in their own bed, and Heidi and I back to Bucksport.

Arriving at the Fort Knox Park Inn, we didn't let the autumn air deter us from taking a late-night walk. As we strolled from streetlamp to streetlamp along the river's edge, I couldn't have thought of a more picturesque spot. The lights of the Penobscot Narrows Bridge reflecting in the water made it appear twice as tall. Posing alongside the majestic Fort Knox, they highlighted the best of what the past and present of this town had to offer.

As Heidi and I continued our walk, we were caught up in the wonders of the day. There had been so many pinch-me moments, we knew tomorrow didn't stand a chance of living up to its predecessor. Resigning ourselves to the fact that the best part of the weekend was over, we walked back toward the hotel.

In the morning, as we entered the Alamo Theater for the second day in a row, we were again greeted with coffee and bagels. The stranger-filled lobby from Friday night had now turned into one of friends on a Sunday morning. As I swallowed my last bite of bagel, my parents and sister returned as promised, and soon we were back in front of the big screen. Without any responsibilities or film to show, the laid-back Sunday morning was a huge contrast to the excitement of the day before. As noontime approached, the final film was just ending and I was having trouble. Without thinking, I had allowed myself to be sandwiched in on both sides of a row without water for my medicine. Now cemented into my seat, it was all I could do to pull myself up and go take my pills.

On my return, everyone was gathering their coats and heading for the lobby. I asked Dad if he was ready to go.

"Whenever you are," he answered back.

With that, we started for the exit. Navigating through the doors, I was soon pushing Dad straight up the sidewalk.

When we arrived at the car, I asked him for the spare keys, the ones he always carried. He informed me that Mother had both sets today. Knowing she probably wasn't far behind, I swung his chair around and pointed Dad toward Main Street so he could watch the traffic.

Leaning against my parents' car, I finally had a little time to think. Now, with the luxury of looking back, I had a deeper understanding of the impact the rescue had had on the world. Five lives were saved that day, and no matter who was rescued or what their age, it was an awesome event. It was truly a story that not only rivals that of Frank Capra's film, *It's a Wonderful Life*, it goes one better: It really happened.

It was hard to believe that the film festival was over and with it, a chapter in my life. It was a journey that had started almost two years before when my biggest mission in life was to just make it through the day. I remembered a cold winter's night sitting in a hospital parking lot. About to get out of my truck, I was facing a world of unknowns: a snow-covered sidewalk with hidden patches of ice, a sickly father who I feared we were about to lose, and a disease that was robbing a little more of me each day. Yet my battle was not just with the outside world; it was being waged inside me between the old man I was fast becoming and the little boy in me that was quickly fading away. Everything was an obstacle, and the things I cherished most seemed to be dying.

When I had come across the newspaper article about the rescue, it was like a hand reaching down into my despair and pulling me to safety. It was the diversion I needed. And as I reached out to the kids

SNOW ANGELS ON THE MOON

who were rescued, it totally surprised me who reached back. Not an author, a doctor, or a lawyer, but kids from a summer camp, thankful for their second chance at life.

The lessons were clear: I couldn't let the little boy in me fade away. Through his eyes, tomorrow is not an obstacle but a clean slate, a second chance at my own life.

The more I told the rescue story, the more of a difference I saw it make in people's lives. My father finally discovered that his life had purpose and meaning. Reunions of long-ago campers were taking place across the country. People hugged their children a little closer, took their parents a little less for granted, and cherished each breath a little more.

As I face tomorrow, I don't know what scares me the most, the knowns or the unknowns. What I do know is that I can't let the *fear* of my disease cripple me before the disease does. My voice, weak and fractured as it sometimes is, is still no less of a voice. And the unsteadiness of my gait, which causes some to look away, can still allow me to stand firm for those treated unjustly.

Preparing to step out into the unknown of Monday morning, I was excited to see what the little boy in me could do with the blank canvas. I wondered if Neil Armstrong had similar thoughts before facing the unknowns of walking on the moon. I can picture him hopping along the lunar surface zigzagging to his next experiment. How could he not help but stop every now and again to make his mark, leaving a trail of snow angels on the moon?

"Russ!" What are you doing out here?" Heidi's voice broke the silence. "Everyone thinks you guys are in the bathroom."

It took me a moment to get my bearings, having just traveled the 238,900 miles from the moon back to a sidewalk in Bucksport, Maine.

"Bathroom? Nope, we're right here," I answered, puzzled as to why they would call out a search party in our honor.

"They just announced that your film won the Audience Favorite Award. They're waiting for you to come out of the bathroom so they can all cheer again." Heidi was all smiles.

"But we're not in the bathroom!" I playfully protested.

GETTING MY BEARINGS

"Just c'mon." Heidi sounded exasperated, as if talking to a child. Which all made perfect sense, because at that moment I was one.

Pushing my father's wheelchair back up the sidewalk toward the Alamo Theater, I couldn't help but zigzag a little along the way.

The End

SOURCES

Bangor Daily News. "Five Saved from Sailboat off Rockland." August 20, 1958.

Blanchard, Jessica. "A Bit of Art Does a School Day Good." *Seattle Post,* Oct 24, 2006.

Boothbay Region Historical Society. Burleigh Hill Camp Folder.

Cheever, Susan. www.susancheever.com.

Children's Hospital & Research Center Oakland. "CHORI scientist Dan Granoff awarded prestigious Maurice Hillman/Merck Award," press release, May 14, 2014.

Courier-Gazette. "David Gamage Cited by Coast Guard Admiral." August 1958.

Everly, Susan. "NY Must Turn on Water." *Associated Press,* November 24, 1970.

Gamage, David A. "Whitehead Light Station—Childhood Memories." *Lighthouse Digest,* August 2000.

Gamage, David A. "Whitehead Light Station." *The Keeper's Log,* Fall 2000.

Goldsmith, Susan. "Fighting a Third World Menace." *East Bay Express* (Oakland, CA), March 2004.

Granoff, Dan. Handwritten journal dated December 10, 1958.

Jeffrey G. Stark Biography, https://www.forchellilaw.com.

Keanelly, Christopher. "The Success of a Late Bloomer." *Los Angeles Times,* November 24, 1985.

Laylan, Peter R., letter to the editor, *Edmonds Beacon,* July 2, 2013.

New York Daily News (*Corpus Christi Times-Caller*). "Boa Eludes Posse of Cautious Police." Sept 3, 1956.

New York Times. "Police Tear Gas Fails in Hunt for Hunt Snake." September 3, 1956l

New York Times. "Sailing Gets a Vote as Top Character Builder." February 16, 1964.

Portland Press Herald. "High Tide, Surf Close York Beach." August 1858.

US Dept of Commerce Weather Bureau. Hurricane Cleo Preliminary Report. August 14–19 1958.

ACKNOWLEDGMENTS

When I began this journey four years ago, I had no idea of the discoveries I would make and the amazing people I would meet along the way. However, it also made me appreciate the people who were already in my life even more. Some were close friends and some stepped out of the past from forty years ago, but all proved to be just as amazing as the people I found. They gave so freely of their time and talents, offering encouragement and kindness along the way.

For those on the frontlines of writing this book, I thank you: Van Reid, who guided me in his craft and helped draw the storyteller out of me; Karen Thompson for her willingness to proofread my galley proof in her overwhelmingly busiest time of the year; Nancy Courville, the warrior, who made me defend my words; and my wife, Heidi, whose contributions could fill the page, but I will keep it simple and just say she is a true believer.

I am forever grateful for my family: My wife, Heidi; my mother, Sandra; my son and son-in-law, Drew Lane and Josh Tolby; my daughter and son-in-law, Amanda and Jon Morningstar; my grandson, Dietrich; my sister and brother-in-law, Becky and Billy Bryant; and my niece and her husband, Lindsay and Luke Plummer.

My dear friends, Jody and Todd Bachelder, David and Kate Bartlett, Jimmy Bartlett, Nancy and John Courville, Ruth Schroeder Halter, Chad and Mary Hanna, Cory Hanna, Bobby Ives, Gigi Lirot, Jay and Lorilee Locke, Van Reid, Cindy and Rendon Sabina, and Karen Thompson, thank you all.